The Cultivation of Body and Mind in Nineteenth-Century American Delsartism

Recent Titles in
Contributions to the Study of Music and Dance

The Cultivation of Body and Mind in
Nineteenth-Century American Delsartism

Nancy Lee Chalfa Ruyter

Contributions to the Study of Music and Dance,
Number 56

GREENWOOD PRESS
Westport, Connecticut • London

Library of Congress Cataloging-in-Publication Data

Ruyter, Nancy Lee Chalfa.
    The cultivation of body and mind in nineteenth-century American
Delsartism / Nancy Lee Chalfa Ruyter.
        p.   cm.—(Contributions to the study of music and dance,
ISSN 0193–9041 ; no. 56)
    Includes bibliographical references (p.   ) and index.
    ISBN 0–313–31042–4 (alk. paper)
    1. Delsarte system—History.   2. Physical education and training—
United States—History—19th century.   3. Dance—United States—
History—19th century.   4. Delsarte, François, 1811–1871.
5. Stebbins, Genevieve.   I. Title.   II. Series.
    GV463.R84   1999
    792'.028—dc21   99–10076

British Library Cataloguing in Publication Data is available.

Library of Congress Catalog Card Number: 99–10076
ISBN: 0–313–31042–4
ISSN: 0193–9041

First published in 1999

Greenwood Press, 88 Post Road West, Westport, CT 06881
An imprint of Greenwood Publishing Group, Inc.
www.greenwood.com

Printed in the United States of America

The paper used in this book complies with the
Permanent Paper Standard issued by the National
Information Standards Organization (Z39.48–1984).

10 9 8 7 6 5 4 3 2 1

Copyright Acknowledgments

The author and publisher gratefully acknowledge permission for the use of the following material:

Extracts from *Delsarte System of Expression*, by Genevieve Stebbins. 1977 Dance Horizons reprint of 6th edition (New York: Edgar S. Werner, 1902). Used by permission of Princeton Book Company.

Charts and their explanations from *Every Little Movement*, by Ted Shawn. 1974 Dance Horizons republication of 2nd revised and enlarged edition (author, 1963). Used by permission of Princeton Book Company.

Material for chapter 9 from "Antique Longings: Genevieve Stebbins and American Delsartean Performance," by Nancy Lee Chalfa Ruyter. In Susan Leigh Foster, ed., *Corporealities: Dancing, Knowledge, Culture and Power* (London: Routledge, 1996). Used by permission of Routledge.

In loving memory of my husband,
Hans Cornelis Ruyter (1922–1998)

Contents

Illustrations follow Part I.

Preface

This project was begun several years ago. One chapter in my book *Reformers and Visionaries: The Americanization of the Art of Dance* (1979) had surveyed American Delsartism, and I realized there was much more to be investigated. In 1983 I resumed the Delsarte work and began conducting research, which took me to a number of libraries in the United States, England, and France. For some of the early work I enjoyed the help of my multilingual husband, who was always ready to collaborate with me on dance research: accompanying me to libraries and helping to ferret out elusive data, working through difficult passages of translation, and discussing points of view and possible directions to follow. In the early years of this research, I was collecting information on every possible aspect of the American Delsartean phenomenon, but to include all of that would have taken even more years to complete and probably would have resulted in an unwieldy work spreading out in too many directions. Some of the omitted but interesting facets of American Delsartism that I have found will have to wait for future articles to see the light of day.

I am indebted to many institutions and individuals for help in gathering information on François Delsarte and his followers. In 1983 I visited the Delsarte Collection, University Archives, Hill Memorial Library at Louisiana State University, Baton Rouge, the most important archive of Delsarte material in Europe or the United States. Research Archivist Gisela J. Lozada and other staff were very helpful during my visit to this collection. During the 1980s with the assistance of Philip Cronenwett,

Curator of Manuscripts and Chief of Special Collections, and Ken Cramer, Archivist of Special Collections, I was able to order photocopies of almost everything in the Steele Mackaye Collection and the Henrietta Hovey material in the Richard Hovey Collection from the Dartmouth College Library, and later, I obtained copies of photographs. In the spring of 1986, I spent a sabbatical leave doing research in Paris at the Bibliothèque Nationale, including the Bibliothèque de l'Arsenal and the Bibliothèque et Musée de l'Opéra, and at the Archives Nationales; and in London at the British Library, then located in the British Museum, and at the Colindale Newspaper Division. I have also done work in Washington, D.C., at the Library of Congress, which holds a surprising amount of material on American Delsartism; and in the Dance and Theater Divisions of the New York Public Library Performing Arts Collection. Last year, Vicki Brewer and others at the Church of Light headquarters in Los Angeles sent me materials from their archives on Genevieve Stebbins and her importance in their historical past. Finally, I wish to note the continuing and valuable service I have received over the years from the library staff at the University of California, Irvine. I have the greatest appreciation for all the assistance these institutions and their staffs have provided.

I wish to thank the University of California, Irvine, for sabbatical leaves and research and travel grants during the many years that I have been working on this project. Particularly important was time off to spend six months (January to June 1993) at the University of California Humanities Research Institute (UCHRI) as a member of the Dance History and Theory Resident Group. My thinking about the American Delsarte phenomenon was stimulated and honed by my challenging colleagues in that group: Susan Leigh Foster, Mark Franko, Lena Hammergren, Peggy Phelan, Heidi Gilpin, Sally Ann Ness, Linda J. Tomko, Randy Martin, and Marta E. Savigliano. I am grateful to them all.

Other colleagues who have contributed suggestions or given leads to information include Selma Landen Odom, Christena L. Schlundt, Naima Prevots, Diane Howe, Michael Huxley, Anna Blewchamp, Marlene Smith-Baranzini, and the late Monique Babsky of Paris. The indomitable Claire de Robilant of London provided me with leads and data that have added considerably to my knowledge, and the Dutch dance historian Nancy de Wilde led me to Hade Kallmeyer's writings.

Alain Porte, who is the leading Delsarte scholar in the world today, has shared much important information and insights with me including a copy of the unpublished genealogy of the Delsarte family that was compiled in 1986 by Simone Delsarte-Portzert, great-granddaughter of François Delsarte, and Porte's own anthology of Delsarte's writings, the first collection and publication of them in the original French. I remember with pleasure discussions with Alain and his research assistant, the dancer and choreographer Jeannette Dumeix, when they were conducting Delsarte research in the United States in 1990.

In Paris, I had the great good fortune to be able to meet one of the descendants of François Delsarte. My husband and I spent a lovely afternoon with Jacqueline Gancel-Bouts, another of Delsarte's great-granddaughters, who discussed her illustrious forebear with us and also permitted us to photocopy the manuscript on Delsarte's life and work that had been written by his daughter (her grandmother), Madeleine.

My gathering, organization, and translation of data on American Delsartism has been greatly facilitated over the years through the work of a number of people—Christene A. Aschan, Research Assistant for the UCHRI; and research assistants who have worked for me in various capacities: Beth Koslin, Dimitry Panesevich, Jane Reifer, Ahmed Valk, Angela Rector, Jocelyn Danchick, Donna Evleth, Phoenix Alexander, and Jennifer Hiller. I thank them all for their contributions to this project.

I am very grateful to Pamela St. Clair, Rebecca Ardwin, and Marsha Havens, of the Greenwood Publishing Group for their expert and skilled assistance in preparing the manuscript for publication.

Finally, I wish to express gratitude to my late husband for his unwavering support of my research endeavors.

Introduction

When twenty or thirty earnest women assemble for their first lesson
in what they vaguely term "Delsarte," I always feel inclined . . . to
ask them why they are there, what incentive leads them to make
such an investment of their time and money. Back of all answers
there is one general motive, namely: a desire for health. Occasionally,
a bright-faced girl says, "I want to be graceful," . . . or a woman says,
"I want to get possession of myself; my body is really an incum-
brance, I never know what to do with it." (Bishop 1892a: 25–26)

It was only here in America, and after Delsarte's death that his laws
were apprehended and used by dancers to revolutionize the art of
the dance . . . [their application] completely changed the calibre, quality and significance of dancing in the 20th century. (Shawn 1974: 61)

These statements by nineteenth-century teacher and writer Emily Bishop
and twentieth-century dance pioneer Ted Shawn represent two aspects
of the phenomenon known as American Delsartism: its use for the improvement of everyday life, on the one hand, and for professional work
in the arts, on the other. The first, which sometimes included amateur
performance, was taken up by countless late-nineteenth-century American women, while the latter has affected dance developments in the
United States and Europe. The Delsartean complex of theory and practice
went from its origins in France as a professional art endeavor (in music
and drama) to a broad-based social phenomenon after transplantation to

the United States, and then back to a limited focus in the arts—this time in dance. Its lay practitioners as well as its professional artists had a strong sense of mission and equated beauty of expression with truth and transcendent experience.

The main goals of this study are to chronicle the history of American Delsartism from the often fragmentary data that is available; to provide biographical information on its major proponents, including its French initiator, François Delsarte; and to explore its range of theory and practice, particularly as realized in the work of Genevieve Stebbins. I am sceptical regarding the historian's ability to pin down the truth about any phenomenon, especially something as ephemeral as bodily movement, but this is such an attempt—with full realization that the story can never be complete and will be revised as new information and interpretive insights appear on the scene. Along the way of narrating what I see as the history of American Delsartism, I consider its role in the lives of nineteenth-century American women and its relevance to the developments that followed in twentieth-century dance. While I would not be writing about this subject if I did not believe it has significance in at least those two contexts, the main purpose of this study is not to situate American Delsartism in the broad sweep of history or to explore it by means of one or another theoretical construct. It is rather to try to determine the "who," "what," "where," and "when" of it, something we have not known—as shown by the frequent inaccurate or incomplete information one finds in many references to Delsarte in dance literature and the lack of attention to it in women's studies. The "why's" are, of course, important, but they take second place here.

One problem with investigating this subject is the difficulty of getting close to it, of trying to imaginatively enter its world. Photographs of American Delsarteans in their versions of Greekish-style gowns, look quaint and somewhat silly as they imitate statues or depict melodramatic scenes from antiquity. If such illustrations had any beauty or power in their own time, it is not apparent to us today. There is no sense of the body within the gown. An acting critic would disparage their gestures as mere "indicating" rather than "expressing." Despite the Delsarteans' attempts at profundity, these images look superficial. Similarly, in our time, much of the writing of American Delsarteans seems pretentious and inane. One wonders if they really believed their enthusiastic goings-on about correspondence between the body and the soul; the godliness of the aesthetic; the nobility of effective expression; and the rigid formulas for the physical rendering of character, moods, and thoughts. One might ask if the physical activities and their intellectual underpinnings constituted an effective discipline for body and mind and the integration of the two. Did the Delsartean work touch anyone deeply? Did it give any of its adherents joy? Or enlightenment? Or a sense of power? Does it equate in any way with present-day approaches to physical, mental, and spiritual growth? Does it have anything in common with our dance or fitness disciplines? How do we, living in the late twentieth century, and with all the possibilities of lifestyle that surround us, come to an understanding of the meaning of the Delsarte work to nineteenth-century middle- and upper-class ladies?

In studying the past we cannot observe or experience what social scientist Paul Connerton has identified as *"incorporating* practice." He defines this as "all the messages that a sender or senders impart by means of their own current bodily activity, the transmission occurring only during the time that their bodies are present to sustain that particular activity" (1989: 72). We are limited in our study to poring over the results of what he calls *"inscribing* practice . . . [what remains when] we do something that traps and holds information, long after the human organism has stopped informing" (1989: 73). I believe Connerton's concept is useful in the consideration of any phenomenon of the past that has bodily practice as its fundamental element. We can usually find written or visual material pertaining to dance, exercise, the presentation of self in various contexts, and so forth. The trick is not to limit ourselves to documenting data from such sources, but to try to find clues in the data that will help us understand (in our own bodies) something of the incorporating practices, and to at least suggest to our readers some of the questions or possibilities raised by the data in relation to bodily experience.

The "inscribing practices" of the American Delsarteans can be found in photographs and some drawings; unpublished manuscripts and notes in archival collections; a plethora of books, articles, and performance scenarios written by proponents, promoters, and an occasional detracter; a few reviews of lecture and performance presentations; and what seems like a million small news items printed in the Delsartean periodical literature. I hope that besides pinning down some of the factual history of American Delsartism, we can use this material to at least speculate on the Delsarteans' physical as well as intellectual experiences with the theory and practice to which they were drawn. Let us ponder if indeed they might have felt something of the integration of body, mind, emotions, and spirit that was promoted in Delsartean and other self-help literature of the nineteenth century and what such an experience might have meant to them.

The life of the middle- and upper-class American women who engaged in Delsartean activities was controlled by beliefs, culture, and customs that are, in some ways, distant from those of the comparable segment of American society today. We are certainly familiar with gender inequity and power differentials, but happily not to the extent of our counterparts in the last century. They belonged to a society that expected them to follow a strict code of behavior. It was a male-dominated society, but this does not mean that the men had a great deal more freedom than the women. Men, of course, had more power and authority and were freer to engage in a variety of activities, but their behavioral limits were also strictly defined. Middle- and upper-class values dictated how people should dress, speak, and exercise their bodies and minds; how they should spend their time and energy; what their attitudes toward sex and their sexual behavior should be; and what standards and strategies for health were appropriate.

Women's lives were restricted by various doctrines promoted by male authorities in education and medicine. These were not universally held, but were pervasive enough to effect the lives of many. Most relevant in this context was the belief that women's physical and mental education should be limited in order not to weaken their reproductive function, that is, their supposed primary reason for existing. As historian Carroll Smith-Rosenberg explains it, "Woman's body, doctors contended, contained only a limited amount of energy—energy needed for the full development of her uterus and ovaries. At the commencement of puberty, then, a girl should curtail all activity" (1986: 187). The curtailment was extreme and clearly embodied a social and political agenda to keep women in their place. Smith-Rosenberg continues: "Indeed physicians routinely used this energy theory to sanction attacks upon any behavior they considered unfeminine; education, factory work, religious or charitable activities, virtually any interests outside the home during puberty were deplored" (1986: 187). There was an obvious fear that if women engaged in activities beyond the traditional role of wife and mother they would not only endanger their capacity to bear and raise children, but also threaten the established social order.

As the nineteenth century progressed, however, American women experienced accelerated changes in their lives and the expansion of opportunities. Increasingly they could explore and venture into new pursuits that had previously been outside of their supposedly proper sphere. Many pushed at the traditional limits that had constrained them in both education and the professional world.[1] At the same time, doctors and physical educators developed new theories and methodologies for the use of exercise in the establishment and maintenance of good health for the whole population.[2] Some of this work was geared primarily for women because their need for exercise had been at best ignored and at worst opposed by the conservative medical establishment.[3] In the 1880s and 1890s, American Delsartism became fashionable in the United States as one component of the reforms that were occurring throughout society. It is not only relevant to the histories of women's education, health, and clothing reform, however, but also is important as one of a number of late-nineteenth-century contexts within which women could assume leadership in the public sphere.

The context for development of American Delsartism was the field of elocution (voice and speech training for public speaking), which had been developing on a national scale from the 1820s.[4] By the late nineteenth century, there were elocutionary schools, performance venues, publications, and a national network of professional associations. From the mid-century on, some elocution instructors increasingly emphasized gesture and bodily motion, and the term "expression" came into vogue for work that included physical culture, pantomine, acting, and interpersonal communication as well as training for the speaker's "platform." Instruction in the narrower field of elocution had originally been an important part of education for men, especially for clergymen, lawyers, public readers, and lecturers. As educational opportunities for women expanded, such training came to be considered useful and appropriate for them as well.

Expression was taught by various methods in the United States, but the best known and ultimately the broadest in application was the American Delsarte system. It comprised theory from the French teacher of acting, singing, and aesthetics, François Delsarte; practical exercises and formulas for expression based on Delsarte's work and that of his student Steele Mackaye; physical training exercises from a variety of sources; and popular performance genres embodying "Delsartean" principles. Transplanted to the United States, Delsarte's "applied aesthetics" was adapted for use in both professional and nonprofessional contexts and spread nationally with the activities of hundreds of teachers and performers. Through Delsartean training, a considerable number of late-nineteenth-century white middle- and upper-class American women and children were able to pay attention to their bodies in a socially acceptable manner, to undergo training in physical and expressive techniques, and even to present themselves to selected audiences in public performances.

By the late nineteenth century one could find the adjective "Delsartean" applied to teachers, schools, performances, and publications—and even to corsets that were less restrictive and harmful than the ones fashionable women had been wearing. As Delsartism spread across the United States, it came to involve thousands of students—mostly women and female children. In addition to furthering the cause of women's physical culture and expression, some proponents also used the aesthetic principles to argue for artistry in everyday life—in clothing, house decor, social interaction, and anything else that might be improved with attention to its aesthetic qualities.

The relevance of American Delsartism to women's social and cultural history has been almost totally ignored. In works on nineteenth-century American women's lives, health, education, and so on, there seems to be little awareness that American Delsartism even existed, let alone any sense of its importance. This is probably partly due to the fact that the

Delsarteans themselves were not typically leaders of the burning issues of the day—causes such as women's suffrage, education, and health. Even in the area of clothing reform, which was espoused by Delsarteans as well as others, there seems to have been little communication between mainstream and Delsartean efforts. Two exceptions to the general absence of attention to the Delsarte movement in its social context appear in the work of Judy Burns, who has tied the American infatuation with Delsartism to themes of women's self-cultivation and image making (see, for example, 1989; 1996); and Richard A. Meckel in his contextualization of American Delsartism as manifested in the career of Henrietta Hovey (1989; he refers to her as Henrietta Russell).

The relevance of the Delsarte theory and practice to the art of dance, on the other hand, has long been recognized. In twentieth-century dance histories, Delsarte is typically mentioned or briefly discussed (for example, see Baril 1984; Joyeux 1981, Martin 1936; Mazo 1977; and Sorell 1986), or treated more extensively such as in Ted Shawn's *Every Little Movement* (1994); Suzanne Shelton's discussions of the influence of American Delsartism on Ruth St. Denis (1978; 1981); Ann Daly's study of Isadora Duncan (1995); Kendall (1979); Thomas (1995); and my own writings on American Delsartism. Similarly, attention has been paid to the role of the Delsarte system in the development of actor training in the United States (see, for example, Aslan 1974; Hodge 1954; McArthur 1984; McTeague 1993; and Wilson 1966).

In the 1990s there has been increasing European interest in Delsarte and his work, especially in its relevance to the art of dance. The Théâtre National de la Danse et de l'Image/Chateauvallon (TNDI) presented a major exhibition at the Museum of Toulon, 21 March to 14 May 1991, and published a catalog that stands as a major document on Delsarte's life and work (Rambaud and Vincent 1991). That exhibition, in a somewhat revised version, was brought to Rimini, Italy, as part of the theatre festival *Santarcangelo dei Teatri XXII* during the summer of 1992. A two-day international conference (4–5 July) focused on the Delsarte system's influence both in Europe and the United States and resulted in a publication (Randi 1993). A major work published in France in 1992 is Alain Porte's *François Delsarte: une anthologie*, which includes historical discussion and a chronology of Delsarte's life in addition to a large selection of Delsarte's writings and statements.

Even with all the attention that has been paid to the relevance of Delsartism to dance history, there is a great deal of information that is simply not known. It hides in archives in this country and abroad and in obscure publications that have been consulted only by a few specialists on the Delsartean phenomenon. I am one of those and hope that this study will provide some basic information and suggest implications and questions that can be further explored for greater understanding of both of the contexts in which the Delsarte system had an impact.

This volume begins with a chapter on François Delsarte and five of his students (including two of his own children) who are relevant to the history of American Delsartism. Chapter 2 focuses on the American theatre practitioner Steele Mackaye, who ushered in the first phase of American Delsartism, and some of his students and colleagues in theatre and related fields. Through the work of these two men and their followers, the highly idealistic foundation of the Delsartean phenomenon was established. They were committed to the creation of art and artists, and saw this not only as merely professional endeavor, but also as moral and spiritual striving. The next three chapters discuss the figures most responsible for adapting the Delsarte material for general as well as specialized training, predominantly for female students. Chapter 3 looks at the life and work of Henrietta Hovey, the first American Delsartean to introduce the system and its practices into the society milieu and the one with the most direct influence on the early history of American modern dance. Chapter 4 explores the life and career of Genevieve Stebbins, the most active leader in the development and dissemination of American Delsartean theory and practice. Finally, in Chapter 5 I survey the spread of Delsartism across the United States and back to Europe, give profiles of a few other notable American Delsarteans, and discuss two German physical educators who studied with Stebbins and incorporated Delsartism into their own teaching.

Part II focuses on Delsartean theory and practice and how they developed in the United States. Chapter 6 discusses the system as theorized and taught by Delsarte and Mackaye. The next three chapters are devoted to what can truly be termed "American Delsartism" as realized in the thought and work of Genevieve Stebbins. The focus is on Stebbins because it was she who developed the system furthest and wrote about it in the most depth and breadth. As she matured, the Delsarte system was but a part of her own total approach to physical culture and expression; nevertheless, it was a core element. Furthermore, Stebbins' writings, teaching, and performance provided a model for American Delsartism as practiced by the hundreds of teachers and performers throughout the United States. Chapter 7 examines the sources Stebbins used in the elaboration of her approach, while Chapter 8 looks at the development of her practical teaching as revealed in her writings. Chapter 9 describes and analyzes the performance genres of American Delsartism as developed and presented by Stebbins. The Epilogue summarizes some of the issues raised in this study and suggests further avenues of investigation that would be useful in the contexts of both dance and cultural history.

PART I

THE CAST OF CHARACTERS IN EUROPE AND THE UNITED STATES

Chapter 1

François Delsarte and His French Students

My dear friend, where do you want us to place him? . . . [T]here are under my control round places for round men, we have oval ones and square ones for oval and square individuals, but in good conscience, what would you do with he who assumes all the forms? Del Sarte [*sic*] is an innovator, and we have no place for him. (a French minister, quoted in Madeleine Delsarte 14)

[W]hat a feast . . . to listen . . . to the sweet reveries, the ecstasies, the loves of times passed. The sincere man who has given us these leisures, François Delsarte, is a learned archeologist and a great singer at the same time; he searches, he divines, and when he has found some hidden beautiful thing, oh marvelous! (Jules Janin, quoted in Harang 1945: 46)

A study of the Delsarte system in relation to any of its permutations must begin with attention to the man who originated it and spent his life working out its applications. But how do we place François Delsarte in the contexts of American cultural history and dance? He himself, of course, had no connection with the former and never gave any indication of even considering dance as one of the arts. One wonders what he might have thought about his fame in the twentieth century, which is now derived largely from recognition of his importance to the history of dance.

François Delsarte was born 19 November 1811 in the small city of

Solesmes in northern France, and died 22 July 1871 in Paris.[1] His father, Jean Nicolas Toussaint Delsarte (b. 1778), was an impractical inventor who reportedly was not only unable to support his family but also squandered his wife's dowry on his projects. François' mother, Albertine Aimée Roland Delsarte, had come from a wealthy family. In desperation over the increasing poverty she and her children were suffering, she left her husband to seek some kind of work and better their situation. She placed her two youngest children, Aimée and Camille, with her mother and set off for Paris with the two older sons, François and Louis. She left the boys in a pension, but as money was not provided for their support, they were in effect, abandoned. At some point she died, and Louis succumbed to pneumonia.[2]

Most published accounts of François' early years elaborate the romantic story of an orphan heroically overcoming great odds to develop his talents in music and drama. What seems reliable is that Delsarte was indeed on his own in Paris at a young age and lived a precarious existence from odd jobs. About 1823 or perhaps somewhat later, he was taken in by an elderly and somewhat eccentric professor of music named Bambini who recognized talent in the young man. Bambini offered Delsarte both a home and musical instruction, eventually advising him to enter the Paris Conservatory for more formal and advanced training. Through the good offices of this mentor, Delsarte was admitted into the Conservatory as a vocal student in July 1826 and provided with some financial support.

Delsarte studied at the Conservatory through the end of 1829, but apparently with scant satisfaction on his part or that of the institution and most of its teachers. In later years, he expressed particular unhappiness with the Conservatory's vocal instruction, and in fact, he believed that it had ruined his own voice during his first six months there. In his independent work, Delsarte would subsequently investigate the physical mechanism of the voice and develop a training methodology based on both scientific and aesthetic principles. Delsarte also criticized the actor training offered at the Conservatory. He felt that it only perpetuated the current professional acting that he found artificial and stilted. Moreover, the instruction was inconsistent, with each teacher promoting his own methods, which typically would differ radically from those of others. Delsarte saw no general principles of aesthetics, expression, or method underlying the training, and also no concern with the qualities of naturalness and believability that he considered important.[3]

Despite his frustrations, however, Delsarte remained at the Conservatory three and one-half years, during which time he came into contact with Adophe Nourrit (1802–1839), the Paris Opera's principal tenor from 1826 to 1837 and the Conservatory's newly appointed professor of lyric declamation.[4] Delsarte participated in the regular Conservatory competitions, and it was with Nourrit on the panel that he won his only award, the second prize in singing in August 1828. The following year Nourrit and two others supported the first prize for Delsarte, but their opinions did not prevail.

After leaving the Conservatory, Delsarte's future did not look promising. Only after persistent efforts did he finally obtain work as a singer or actor at the Opéra-Comique, the Théâtre Ambigu, and the Variétés. Despite receiving wages under his contracts, he reportedly performed only infrequently, which gave him time to further develop his emerging theories of artistic expression. In September 1833, at the age of 22, Delsarte published his first formal statement on singing, *Méthode philosophique du chant* (reprinted in Porte 1992). That same year he married a nearly 16-year-old fellow musician, Rosine Charlotte Andrien (1817–1891), a piano student at the Conservatory.

In 1834 Delsarte left the lyric stage altogether. His voice was perhaps too seriously impaired for regular performing, but there were undoubtedly other reasons as well. From Delsarte's own testimony as well as that of his daughter Madeleine, it is apparent that he was not a man ready to compromise to get on in the world. He was committed to the truth as he saw it. Finding much to criticize in the musical and theatrical institutions of his day, he apparently had no qualms about expressing his opinions to anyone—whether they were of high or low status. Such unwavering commitment to his own principles may well have contributed to his lack of success on the professional stage.

Despite the impairment of his voice, however, Delsarte performed regularly in his own concerts from 1839 to 1866 (when he was 55 years old). In such a setting, where he himself had complete control, he apparently sang very well. He could choose the musical selections and the style of presentation that would both protect his voice from further damage and illustrate his principles of expression and vocal production. His concerts typically featured work of the seventeenth- and eighteenth-century masters, Gluck, Rameau, Lulli, Handel, and Mozart, music that had been largely ignored by the nineteenth-century French music establishment.

In his choice of songs to perform, Delsarte favored dramatic material that required both acting and vocal ability. Critics consistently expressed admiration and respect for his choice of repertoire, the skill and beauty of his vocal quality, and his expression of words, character, emotion, and action in relation to the music. For example, in 1853, Jules-Gabriel Janin, noted Parisian drama and literary critic, reviewed one of Delsarte's concerts:

> It would not be easy to recount the joy and the pleasure of that intimate evening. . . . [T]he poise, the movement, the agitation, the wisp of laughter; one cannot recount the happy

> contentment of a crowd of discreet gentlemen, fine judges,
> enthusiastic and good pupils who begin to listen with a sort
> of filial piety to the forgotten masterpieces which were for-
> merly the grace and the charm of their ancestors. (quoted in
> Harang 47)

Janin particularly praised Delsarte's performance of the Clytemnestra
scene from Gluck's *Iphigénie en Aulide* (1774, based on the Racine play of
1675): "Ah! what energy and what beauty! and how the verses of Racine
have merited the honor that the old Gluck has done to them! Here Delsarte sings as Talma declaimed" (Harang 47). François-Joseph Talma
(1763–1826) had been considered the leading tragedian of his day, so this
was great praise indeed.

One critic, G. W. Barry, noted in 1860 that "Delsarte does not separate
song from declamation, the singer from the actor. For him, a song must
be a sort of tragic chant, where the voice, gestures and countenance co-
operate in the interpretation of the drama" (quoted in Harang 58). Delsarte's range was appreciated by the esteemed composer, musician,
dramatist, and critic Henri Blanchard, who wrote in May 1858:

> He personifies and perfects, . . . the humanity of the animals
> of the fables of Fontaine through his picturesque declamation,
> true and with an excellent comic art. [And going on to another
> piece:] Is there anything more touching than the manner in
> which he recites musically the romance of Joseph? He makes
> it an elegy full of tears. (quoted in Harang 52–53)

Delsarte also presented his pupils in these concerts, and they too received
enthusiastic praise from the critics.

In addition to his concert work, Delsarte taught singing and declamation, based on his own developing system. He had begun to formulate
ideas about training and expression in the arts during his Conservatory
years. He focused on two related areas: the narrower issues of vocal and
acting theory, practice, and training; and the broader theme of general
aesthetics and expression in any art medium. He taught on two levels:
private lessons and small classes in declamation or singing, and a series
of lectures—his *Cours d'esthétique appliquée*—on his philosophical and
aesthetic theory.

In 1839, at age 28, Delsarte gave the first of these series of lectures.
While he had probably already engaged in some private teaching, this
was the formal opening of his school. According to his pupil Angélique
Arnaud, Delsarte's "Course of Applied Aesthetics was addressed to

painters, sculptors, orators, as well as to musicians, both performers and composers; and was finally extended to literary men" (1893: 201).[5]

From 1839 to 1859, Delsarte was at the height of his powers and received great acclaim for his theoretical work, his teaching, his reintroduction of old music, and his own artistry. Beginning in 1860, when he was 49, Delsarte's health began to fail and he went into semi-retirement, although he still taught and performed on a limited basis.

François and Rosine Delsarte had seven children,[6] and, according to Madeleine, they all at least informally learned their father's system of expression as well as acquired music training from their mother. There is record of only Gustave and Marie actually teaching the Delsarte system, however, and that seemed to be on a limited basis. Apparently Delsarte envisioned Xavier as his ultimate successor, but that young man's untimely death from cholera in 1863 shattered that hope.

In the touching memoir written after her father's death, Madeleine characterized Delsarte as a "man of genius" and an "implacable enemy of routine" with an encyclopedic mind and a voracious curiosity and appetite for research (14). In addition to the aspects of his work that attracted the interest of late-nineteenth-century Americans (his system of expression and aesthetic theory), Delsarte also devoted energy and time to drawing; to musical composition; to critical editions of the early music that he reintroduced into the Paris musical scene; and to mechanical inventions such as the phonopticon, a device for tuning musical instruments.

Delsarte's intensity, passion, and absolute commitment to his own views exacted a heavy price from both himself and his family—not to mention any of the rest of the world who came into conflict with him. He seemed to be extreme in everything. He insisted that whatever he cared about must be exactly as he dictated (whether this involved the preparation of his food, the chaotic disarray of his papers, or the accompaniment of his singing). As Madeleine wrote, "He did not tolerate his convictions being attacked" (16). While he was disdainful of the rich and powerful—especially if they demonstrated a pretentious attitude, he would sacrifice his own time and meager financial resources to help the humble or needy student or hanger-on. Despite his punctiliousness in some matters, he was so careless of social obligations that he would forget important engagements and so absent-minded about dress that he might go visiting in his house slippers. His nervousness about performing was intense. According to Madeleine, "he didn't appear once in public without being congested, seized with dizziness and migraine" (15). If he chose not to perform, however, he might at the last minute cancel an engagement or send his young son Xavier in his place. Madeleine wrote that her father "was a curious mixture of vehemence and apathy, of violence and weakness, of terrible angers and almost feminine tendencies'' (19). What seems clear, however, from her memoir and the writings of others who knew him is that he was a warm-hearted and affectionate man despite his eccentricities.

Unfortunately, Delsarte never completed—in fact, he barely started— the full exposition of his discoveries and conclusions, which he described in an undated letter to the king of Hanover (to whom he wished to dedicate the book). It was to be entitled "My Revelatory Episodes, or the History of an Idea Pursued for Forty Years." Notes for this projected book and for some of his lectures as well as the entire address he gave at the Sorbonne in 1865 were translated for American readers beginning in the 1880s and appeared in publications such as Delaumosne's *Delsarte System of Oratory* (from 1885, 3rd edition, on) and Stebbins' *Delsarte System of Expression* (beginning with the 1887 2nd edition), and again in Zorn's twentieth-century compilation. Much of this material is now available in the original French in Alain Porte's volume.

When Delsarte died in 1871, his illustrious career and accomplishments were noted in some 29 obituary notices in the French press. He was characterized as an "eminent professor of voice and declamation," a "great artist," and a "man of genius" (Harang 73, 80, 84).

François Delsarte's lifelong goal had been to discover and then teach what he came to believe were the scientific principles of expression in the arts. There is also some evidence that he had strong feelings about the role of the arts in society. Even after completing his studies at the Conservatory, Delsarte's association with Adolphe Nourrit seems to have continued in their joint espousal, along with fellow musicians and artists, of the Saint-Simonian utopian-socialist movement. This had developed in France ca. 1825–1835 and its influence extended further into the nineteenth century. As one aspect within their broad-ranging program, the Saint-Simonians urged serious purpose and social responsibility in the arts rather than their creation purely for entertainment. One report, suggesting Delsarte's interest in Saint-Simonianism (at least for a time), notes that he and Nourrit had considered collaborating on a popular theater institution that would be based on idealistic and religious principles—a plan that was never realized (Locke 1986: 100). The Saint-Simonians valued the works of composers such as Gluck and Mozart. They appreciated the serious intent in this music, which is what they wished to promote in the arts of their own day (Locke 58–59, 98–99, 120, 205), and as we have seen, Delsarte was known for presenting this type of music.

It is interesting that Delsarte passionately pursued expressive truth in his theory and practical work with singers and actors and placed great emphasis on physical expression in his teaching. Yet he seemed totally unaware or uninterested in applying his principles to the ballet and its artists. He could hardly have been unaware of dance, particularly since he had worked on and performed songs in his own concerts from the title role of the 1831 opera *Robert le diable* (Arnaud 1893; 348–49; Madeleine Delsarte 51–55). At the Paris Opera, this role had been created and was regularly performed by Delsarte's mentor Nourrit (Locke 97). The opera featured the "Ballet of the Nuns," a seminal opus of the Romantic ballet, and it is unlikely that Delsarte would not have seen it and been aware of it as a noteworthy innovation. His writings and course lectures, however, make no mention of that or any other ballet.

From the other side, of course, there is no indication that contemporary ballet choreographers and dancers had any awareness of or would have been interested in the quality of expression that Delsarte promoted. If he had been around in the days of Noverre and Viganò, the situation might well have been different as they were concerned with expression and communication through pantomime and gesture. Even though stories, pantomime, and emotion filled the Romantic era ballets, the emphasis was on the beauty and the virtuosity of the movement rather than what it was meant to convey in a literal sense.

DELSARTE'S STUDENTS

Over the years, Delsarte had taught noted nineteenth-century singers such as Caroline Carvalho, Pauline Gueymard, Marie Malibran, and Henriette Sontag; actors such as Madeleine Brohan, Marie Pasca, and Rachel; and well-known writers, composers, churchmen, lawyers, and painters (Dillport). After Delsarte's death, five of his French students carried forward his work and directly or indirectly influenced the development of Delsartism in the United States. These were the Abbé Delaumosne, Angélique Arnaud, Delsarte's son Gustave and daughter Marie, and Alfred Giraudet.

Abbé Delaumosne

The Abbé Delaumosne was an obscure priest from a small parish outside Paris who had studied with Delsarte during the late 1850s or early 1860s.[7] He has been described by a student of Gustave Delsarte's as a tall, erect man with a commanding presence, a "profound student" but "one of the worst speakers" the writer had ever heard (Odend'hal). He was a close friend of the Delsarte family and apparently had much affection for them. He probably lived until at least 1897.

Delaumosne's book, *Pratique de L'art Oratoire de Delsarte*, was published in Paris in 1874 and in English translation in New York in 1882 as the *Delsarte System of Oratory*. It was not particularly valued by others knowledgeable about Delsarte's system. Alfred Giraudet, for example, criticized it as "imperfect, and often inexact, delusive in its obscurity and even unintelligible." He claimed that Delaumosne attended Delsarte's lectures in 1861 only "from time to time, as a mere *spectator* and *listener*" (1885: 10). Delsarte's daughter, Marie Géraldy, on her visit to the United States, characterized it as "an expression of love for his dead friend," and added that "while he was not a particularly brilliant or erudite man, he was a devoted admirer and pupil of Delsarte, and also a firm friend of the family, whom he thought to please by his work" (quoted in "Delsartiana" June 1892: 160). The American elocutionary leader Moses True Brown (see Chapter 2), who based his own teaching on Delsarte, gave it a mixed review. While, in his opinion, Delaumosne had omitted some essentials and injected too much "theological color," the cleric had clearly presented the "central feature of Delsarte ... *the immanence of the essence or soul, in the substance or body*, and the *three modes of motion by which the inner manifests itself in the outer* (1882b: 74). Whatever its shortcomings Delaumosne's book offered Americans the first detailed published account of the Delsarte system and stimulated interest in it, discussions about it, and further publications on it.

The Abbé's treatise includes a biographical sketch of Delsarte, followed by several chapters devoted to each of Delsarte's basic agents of expression: voice, gesture, and speech. In the section on gesture, Delaumosne follows his master closely in terms of theory, structure, and content, providing ninefold charts illustrating aspects of facial expression, hand gestures, positions of the feet in standing, and what he calls "Criterion of Chorography [*sic*]," a chart that shows possible designs or pathways of hand gestures for various expressive purposes. While Delaumosne's book was familiar to untold numbers of Americans, there is a record of only one, Genevieve Stebbins, who managed to meet the man himself.

Angélique Arnaud

Angélique Arnaud (1799–1884), a noted writer and feminist, attended Delsarte's courses in applied aesthetics, probably in the late 1850s.[8] She apparently also participated in the practical work since one fellow student in Paris commented on how, in the early 1860s, she "used to sing the soprano solos, and what a voice she had, and what a beautiful woman she was!" (Odend'hal). The obituary published in *The Voice* (August 1884: 135) describes her as "a woman of remarkable talent and strength of character" who, while "thoroughly [fulfilling] the domestic duties of wife and mother," did not limit herself to that sphere. Besides her writing, she was active in many humanitarian causes such as the Society for the Amelioration of the Condition of Women. In the early 1830s she had also been drawn to the Saint-Simonian movement.

Her publications, dating from 1834 to 1882, include novels, short stories, newspaper articles, pamphlets, and biographies of at least one public figure—François Delsarte. She actually wrote two studies of Delsarte, the first of which is rarely mentioned. She published the second, *François Del Sarte; Ses découvertes en esthétique, sa science, sa méthode,* at the age of 83, and it became a major text in both France and the United States. It was translated into English and published in somewhat edited form in the 1884 second edition of *Delsarte System of Oratory.*

Arnaud's work includes biographical sections on Delsarte's life, religion, friends, students, musical compositions, lecture demonstrations and inventions. There are additional chapters on the theoretical foundations of Delsarte's "science"; his method; whether he could be considered a philosopher; his course of applied aesthetics; his law (or principles) of aesthetics in the context of aesthetic thought throughout history; the elements of art (the True, the Good, the Beautiful); and application of the law of aesthetics to dramatic, lyric, and oratorical arts, literature, architecture, and sculpture.

Gustave Delsarte

Gustave Delsarte (1836–1879) made his debut near the end of May 1856 at one of his father's regular concerts. His conducting of a four-part chorus in medieval songs was heralded as "a happy debut and one which permits the belief that G. Delsarte will uphold honorably the reputation of the one whose instruction and works he must perpetuate" (quoted in Harang 51). Gustave pursued a career as a singer and composer, but unfortunately without much distinction. In her volume on Delsarte, Arnaud wrote that Gustave's few compositions had merit, but that his potential for success as a concert singer and teacher was never realized because of "an ill-assorted marriage and his misanthropic character" (1882: 299).

It is not known whether or not Gustave taught his father's system while the elder Delsarte was still alive. In any case, from right after François' death in 1871, and apparently continuing until his own death in 1879, Gustave *was* teaching, and numbered among his pupils two who would become Delsartean leaders in the United States: William R. Alger and Henrietta Hovey. Alger praised Gustave's teaching and described some aspects of it:

> [H]e taught, as imparted to him by his father, the same system of expression, the same laws and rules, the same gymnastic training, given at a subsequent date by Mr. Mackaye to his pupils, and, still later, published by Miss Stebbins in her books. He taught . . . "spiral movements of the arms" [and] spirations of the whole body, with flowing oppositions of the head, the torso, and the limbs. He trained his pupils in the

gentle, slow, precise expansion, contraction, and modulation of all the expressive agents through their nine forms of attitude, with their interchanging play. He also exemplified the poses of the famous classic statues, with a musical melting out of one into another, without any break in the passage; besides portraying, in the manner of his father, as he said, a great many other poses and movements based directly on their originating principles. (1894: 4)

This was written in the context of a controversy over who had first developed the "aesthetic gymnastics" associated with American Delsartism—François Delsarte or Steele Mackaye. Hovey, who studied with Gustave for six months to a year in the late 1870s, also praised Gustave's teaching—and entered into the fray of this argument (Adams 1894; Hovey 1881). She romanticized the younger Delsarte as "a divine man with many very human imperfections" and as "the saddest man [she] ever knew—a man whose ideals were where there was no hope of his life ever reaching."[9] Lucien Odend'hal, who claimed to have been the last student of Gustave, described him as "the best of fellows" but "like his father, always in debt" (1900: 509).

Marie Géraldy

Delsarte's daughter Marie (b. 1848) was singing in her father's concerts from at least the age of 14, and according to one critic, she "sang with a perfect method and a charming voice" (quoted in Harang 62). Arnaud has written that "Marie learned while very young to reproduce with marvelous skill what were called *the attitudes* and the physiognomy changes" (1893: 298). Odend'hal, on the other hand, disparaged her abilities as merely making "mechanically eighty-one expressions of the eyes, one after the other." Despite her meticulously mastered skills, he did not think she had any special interest in the work (1900: 509).

Mme. Géraldy made a brief visit to the United States in February 1892, giving a lecture at the Berkeley Lyceum in New York, a course of seven lessons on what she considered the fundamental aspects of her father's system, and two lessons on the rendering of fables (all published in *Delsarte System of Oratory*, 533–60). She was described at that time as "a tall, dark-haired, middle-aged woman with an interesting face and a charming French manner" (Woodward 562).

Géraldy expressed great distress at what American Delsarteans taught as her father's system. Twenty years had passed since Mackaye's introduction of Delsarte's ideas in the United States, and the practical work had been adapted to new contexts and had accrued methodology attuned to new purposes. The theory was still intact, but the emphasis on physical culture and nonverbal theater forms was utterly foreign to this daughter, who apparently was trying to maintain her father's system just as she had learned it more than 30 years before. The Americans, in their turn, were disappointed in her. They expected great enlightenment from the daughter of the master. Far from that, they found her repertoire of material thin and uninspiring. Her visit fed the controversy over what was "true" Delsartism.[10]

Alfred Giraudet

Alfred Giraudet (1845–1911) made his debut as a singer in 1866 and performed at the Paris Opera from 1880 until 1883. He became a professor at the Paris Conservatory in 1888.[11] Giraudet had studied with Delsarte for five years (probably from 1861 to 1866), regularly attending both lectures and lessons. He credited Delsarte completely for his success: "My artistic rank in Paris for nearly 20 years, I owe entirely to the Delsarte System. I have never had any other method and have, therefore, of course, been forced to put its principles into practical application and to prove their value to the public" (1885: 9; see also Charles). In addition to his performing career, Giraudet taught singing and declamation on the basis of Delsarte's theory, beginning in 1867.

In 1892 Giraudet opened a school in Paris for instruction in "lyric and dramatic art" based on the Delsarte system. He advertised the academy in *Werner's Voice Magazine* and reportedly was successful in attracting a number of American students. In 1895 Giraudet published his treatise on the Delsarte system, *Mimique, physionomie et gestes; Méthode pratique. D'après le système de F. Del Sarte*. While it was advertised in *The Voice* and there seems to have been some idea of translating it for publication in the United States, it never appeared in English, and so would have little or no impact on the American scene. In any case, by the time it was published in France, the American Delsarte rage was beginning to wind down. In the twentieth century, the indefatigable Ted Shawn with difficulty tracked down a copy of this book and had it translated for his own use. He provided a thorough review and assessment of it in the 1963 second edition of *Every Little Movement: A Book about François Delsarte*. While finding considerable value in Giraudet's volume, Shawn was somewhat disappointed because it was limited to only certain aspects of the Delsarte system (Shawn 1963: 102–18).

In various ways, these five French students of Delsarte contributed to the understanding and development of the Delsarte system in the United States. In their teachings and writings, they presumably tried to present the material exactly as they understood it from Delsarte himself. There is no indication that they or any others in France explored its potential in new directions as the American Delsarteans would do. It is interesting to note that, like their mentor, none of them had any interest in or even apparent awareness of dance. They were all involved in expression in the rendering of verbal texts.

After Delsarte's death, there was no new creative surge, and interest in his work simply died out in his native land. It was only briefly in the 1950s and now more intensely in the 1980s and 1990s that the French have developed a renewed interest in Delsarte—particularly in the historical significance of his work to the development of twentieth-century dance.

In the next chapter we will consider the career and work of James Steele Mackaye, who also was primarily concerned with verbal expression. His emphasis on the physical, however, began to move the Delsarte system in the direction of the nonverbal arts.

NOTES

1. Unless otherwise noted, biographical information is taken mainly from the following sources: Madeleine Delsarte; Porte; Arnaud; Curtiss; Harang; and Durivage. Among these and other biographical accounts, there are inconsistencies regarding data such as Delsarte's birth and death dates, his childhood, and his years of study at the Conservatory. The dates given in this work have been verified by documents in the Archive de France and the Archives Departmentale de la Seine and the more reliable obituary notices in the Harang thesis cited above.

2. The children left with their grandmother fared much better. François' surviving brother Camille eventually became a musician, performing as first tenor in the Rheims opera company and teaching, before finally moving to Australia. Their sister Aimée (b. 1815) joined François and his family in Paris in 1837 where she met her future husband, Adolphe-Amand Bizet, a hairdresser turned singing teacher. For a time, the Bizet and Delsarte families were close and the composer Georges Bizet, son of Aimée and Adolphe-Amand, studied with Delsarte in the mid-1850s (Curtiss 1958).

3. Delsarte discusses his conservatory training in his 1865 "Address before the Philotechnic Society of Paris." See Stebbins 1902; and Arnaud's chapter on this address, "Delsarte before the Philotechnic Association," *Delsarte System of Oratory*, 361–371.

4. Information on Nourrit comes from Robinson 1980; and Locke 1986: 97–101.

5. See also Levy for notes from a student of 1859; and Harang, 53–55, for two reviews of the course: Charles Boissière, "Cours d'Esthétique Apliquée, par F. Delsarte," *La Réforme Musicale*, 23 May, 1858; and "Clôture de Cours de F. Delsarte," *La Réforme Musicale*, 11 July 1858.

6. The name regularly used by each is italicized: *Henri* François (b. 1834), Adrien *Gustave* (1836–1879), Charles Louis *Adrien* (b. 1837), *Xavier* Jean (1844–1863), *Marie* Anne (b. 1848), François Joachim or André (b. 1851, died in childhood), and Marie-*Madeleine* (1853–1927) (Delsarte-Portzert Genealogy).

7. A few words on Delaumosne can be found in Giraudet 1885; and S. S. Curry, undated typed manuscript, Delsarte Papers, Louisiana State University, Box 7, Folder 114, p. 9.

8. Biographical information from *Dictionnaire de Biographie Francaise*, vol. 3, p. 786 (Paris: Librairie Letouzey et Ane, 1939); Dillport 52–54; Marie Deraismes, "Obituary. Mme. Angelique Arnaud," *The Voice* 6 (August 1884): 135.

9. Ted Shawn Collection, New York Public Library Performing Arts Libraries, Dance Collection, Folder #723, Part XIII of Henrietta Hovey mss.

10. See, for example, Coyrière 1892; Bishop 1892a: Appendix; F. W. Adams 1892b; Woodward 1893; and "Delsartiana," May 1892 and June 1892.

11. Biographical information from Bibliotheque de l'Opéra, Paris; Nast 118–33; Charles 1892.

Chapter 2

Steele Mackaye and His American Followers

When he first appeared publicly in this country, . . . [he] was in the splendour of an Adonis-like youth: his eyes sparkling, his cheeks bright, his individuality wholly winning. . . . [H]e had a poet's love of art for beauty's sake. He preached this love of art, and he illustrated his precepts by fair forms and phrases that sank deeply into the minds of even the unsusceptible. (*Star*, 1 January 1888, quoted in P. Mackaye 1:174)

This theatre will be a school for the player and the public, having no less a purpose than the elevation of both. If pure dramatic art retains any of the potency which the pulpit and the press have always urged in its behalf, then this experiment becomes one of social no less than esthetic importance. (Steele Mackaye 1871: 8)

Delsarte's theories were first presented in the United States by his only American student, James Morrison Steele Mackaye (1842–1894), noted American actor, dramatist, director, theatre inventor, and teacher.[1] Prior to his meeting with Delsarte, Mackaye had studied drawing and painting in the United States and Europe, taught art, acted, developed concepts and exercises for pantomime and dramatic expression—and served in the Union Army during the Civil War. He was apparently very accomplished in all of his art activities and encouraged by the masters with whom he studied.

By 1869 Mackaye had concluded that theater was the direction he wished to pursue and he decided to seek further training and knowledge about acting from the great François-Joseph Regnier (1807–1885), noted French actor and distinguished professor at the Paris Conservatory. To this end, he embarked with his family for an extended stay in Paris. Steele's sister had been studying singing with Delsarte and their father, Colonel James Morrison Mackaye, urged his son to consider working with the same teacher. Despite Steele's reluctance, Colonel Mackaye finally convinced him to at least talk to Delsarte.

Reportedly, as soon as they met, the two men felt an instant rapport. Coincidentally, Mackaye bore an uncanny resemblance to Delsarte's late son Xavier whose premature death had shattered his father's hopes for a successor within the family. Mary Medberry Mackaye, Steele's wife, later wrote, "Delsarte found in the quick comprehension and ardent appreciation of this young American a mental and spiritual as well as physical likeness to his beloved son which awoke once more his own hopes and enthusiasms" (quoted in P. Mackaye 1:135). Mackaye was equally taken with Delsarte. According to his wife, he came home from that first meeting "walking on air, wrapped in a mantle of enthusiasm, reverence and delight, which from that day to his latest hour he never relinquished" (quoted in P. Mackaye 1:134). Mackaye postponed study with Regnier to begin daily lessons with Delsarte. They worked together from October 1869 until July 1870 when the Franco-Prussian War forced the Mackaye family to leave Paris.

When Mackaye began his studies with Delsarte, he was not an unsophisticated beginner. According to his son and biographer, Percy Mackaye, he had been interested in expression, pantomime, gymnastics, and aesthetics for almost a decade before meeting Delsarte, even though his first ambition had been to pursue painting as a profession. Percy refers to a document from 1861 to prove the point. It is a daily schedule entitled "Pantomime and Expression," which includes, in addition to four hours of drawing and painting, two hours of "dramatic exercises" with 20 minutes devoted to each of the following: voice, body, pantomime, calisthenics, emotional expressions of countenance, and other exercises (P. Mackaye 1:91). Such preparation would serve Steele Mackaye well in his work with Delsarte and for his future in the theater.

Full mastery of the complexities of the system as taught by Delsarte apparently took years to accomplish. Alfred Giraudet, for example, had studied with Delsarte for five years, and this length of time was probably typical. Steele Mackaye, however, grasped the principles and the specifics unusually fast, and after only a few months of study, Delsarte invited him to assist in teaching the classes and to incorporate his own methodology in the process. More than 20 years later, in 1892, Mackaye wrote the following account of how he had worked with Delsarte in 1869–1870:

Delsarte knew nothing of Harmonic Gymnastics. He taught a series of gestures which were very beautiful and expressive in character—but exceedingly intricate and difficult of imitation. Many of his pupils devoted years to their mastery, and yet failed to completely understand and obey their subtleties. I did this completely to the amazement of Mr. Delsarte in three months. I succeeded by the most diligent study in analyzing the motions according to a system which I invented myself—after analyzing the motions I discovered by close study the physical obstacles existing in my own organization to the realization of these motions in my own action. Before Delsarte and I parted, I had laid the foundation of my whole system and philosophy of psychologic gymnastics of which Harmonic Gymnastics is a branch. While I was with Delsarte I lectured . . . and taught many of his pupils his series of gestures—applying my own system of training to them with results that excited the greatest astonishment and the deepest enthusiasm in Delsarte. He realized that I could understand and apply all that he taught—That I, too, was creative and philosophic. He recognized me as his fellow—in artistic work—called me his only disciple[—]accepted me as his colaborer—and successor.[2]

Mary Medberry Mackaye has noted that from the beginning, Delsarte and Mackaye had been functioning thus, as colleagues as well as in a master-pupil relationship. The hours they spent together each day, she wrote, "were almost equally divided between practical training—wherein was applied the principle already formulated—and the search together after more light, newer and larger applications of known truths, simpler and more direct means of reaching desired results" (M. M. Mackaye 1892: 88).

Upon leaving Paris in July 1870, Mackaye had expected to return in a short time to continue his studies and collaboration with Delsarte. The war, unfortunately, lasted until May 1871. By September 1870, the Mackaye family had made their way back to the United States. There they discovered that news of the Delsarte system had actually preceded their own arrival. An American journalist, Francis Durivage, serving as foreign correspondent in Paris, had visited one of Delsarte's last classes in July 1870 where he observed both Mackaye and Delsarte in action. His enthusiastic letter to a friend in Boston (that was then shared with others) stimulated the interest of two prominent Bostonians whose own enthusiasm for the Delsarte system would be a crucial element in its success in the United States: Professor Lewis Baxter Monroe, dean of the Boston University School of Oratory, and Reverend William Rounseville Alger, a Unitarian minister and author. They traveled to New York to meet Mackaye, to learn more about what seemed to be a crucial breakthrough in the theory and teaching of expression, and to develop plans to promote the system in the United States (from M. M. Mackaye mss. as quoted in P. Mackaye 1:138, 141–42). The three new friends also sought ways to immediately send help to Delsarte, who was in dire need as a result of the war. They managed, with Alger's assistance to get 2,000 francs wired to France and delivered to Delsarte, who had retreated to his birth city of Solesmes to avoid the dangers of wartime Paris. Their long-range plan, however, was to develop a substantial fund to bring Delsarte and his family to the United States and establish an American school of expression under his direction (P. Mackaye 1:142–45).

On 21 March 1871 in Boston, Mackaye gave the first of a series of lectures on the Delsarte system. This was the result of an invitation from the governor of Massachusetts, William Claflin, and 17 other distinguished (and, of course, male) political figures, educators, and writers to present an "illustrative lecture . . . showing especially the connection of the laws of dramatic expression, in the system of Delsarte, with character, morality, esthetics and religion" (quoted in P. Mackaye 1:149–50). The Delsarte system in America thus began its life in a grandiose idealistic sphere, following the lead of Delsarte himself. The lecture drew an enthusiastic crowd of 200 to 300, was well covered in the press, and established Mackaye's reputation as a lecturer, actor, and carrier of a new truth to the New World.

The presentation included lecturing, recitation of dramatic passages to illustrate points he was making, and a demonstration of what Mackaye called the "gamuts of expression." It was not as sober as one might imagine from the wording of the invitation. The critic of the *Boston Advertiser* characterized Mackaye's expressions as "so astonishing and impressive as to beggar all description" and then went on to note Mackaye's changes of emotion:

> running through satisfaction, pleasure, tenderness and love to adoration, and having retraced his steps, [descending] facially through dislike, disgust, envy and hate to fury. . . . [then] transitions from repose to jollity, silliness and prostration, to utter drunkenness; . . . passing through all the grades of mental disturbance to insanity, and down all the stairs of mental weakness to utter idiocy.

He summed up, "The impression produced was at once very lively and very profound" (*Boston Transcript* and *Boston Advertiser* 22 March, 1871, quoted in P. Mackaye 1:151–52).

Mackaye gave other such presentations both to promote interest in the system and to generate revenue, but the plan to bring his mentor to the United States was never realized. Delsarte died 22 July 1871. The implantation and development of the Delsarte work was now in the hands of its three American enthusiasts, Mackaye, Monroe, and Alger. Mackaye continued to lecture in Boston and New York (important centers of oratory and expression) and elsewhere. His most important and influential accomplishment, however, was the conception and development of institutionalized schooling in the actor's art. Indeed, as one historian has claimed, "There is little doubt that Steele Mackaye was the most important single influence in the establishment of formal actor training in this country" (Hodge 558).

Prior to the 1870s, prospective American actors learned by doing, joining stock companies, imitating exemplary models, and deciding individually what they needed to work on and how to learn what was required. Mackaye compared the chaotic situation in his own country with the example of the Paris Conservatory where he had originally intended to study in 1869 and where he did begin studies in August 1872. The example of this institution, coupled with his profound belief in the collaborative teaching he had done with Delsarte, undoubtedly contributed to the conception of his first "school," a three-month course at the St. James Theater in the beginning of 1872. The prospectus sets forth the aspiration of raising the moral as well as artistic level of theatrical literature, performers, and audience members through structured training. It states that

> we can never be sure of fine performers until we can offer such opportunities of education for the profession as will induce people of superior moral character and natural intelligence to go upon the stage. And here we come face to face with the fact that there is not in existence such a thing as a dramatic school or college for the English drama. All attempts to elevate the stage must, of necessity, begin with this. (S. Mackaye 1871: 2)

This was the first of several schools and theatres devoted to the training of actors in what might be termed the Delsarte-Mackaye system (on Mackaye's schools, see McTeague 17–19, 41–43; Hodge 558–61). While Mackaye's lack of practical business sense prevented stability or longevity in any of his theatre or school projects, they were still a major influence on theatre, declamation, and, as it would turn out, physical culture and eventually dance.

Mackaye possessed a keen and creative intellect that allowed him to build on what he had learned from Delsarte and to effectively incorporate his findings from years of thinking about and working with expression. While his work always remained close in theory to that of his mentor, it is with Mackaye that the distinction begins between the Delsarte system as taught in France and American Delsartism. Most importantly, Mackaye either invented or substantially elaborated the series of physical exercises that became an integral part of the American Delsarte system. Throughout his life, Mackaye paid only a little more attention to the art of dance than Delsarte had, but he did display a continuing and avid interest in the physical aspects of the actor's art and training and even offered some dance courses for actors in his training schools.

For the rest of his life Steele Mackaye taught, performed, and directed on the basis of the theory and methodology he had shared with Delsarte; he thereby influenced a generation of teachers and practitioners in theater, oratory, and physical culture.

MACKAYE'S STUDENTS AND COLLEAGUES

The first generation of American Delsarteans who began their study with Mackaye fall into two professional groups: leaders in the field of oratory and theatre and those who specialized in physical culture and nonverbal performance forms including dance. Monroe and Alger were particularly instrumental in helping Mackaye introduce the system to the first group, and contributed to its broad dissemination in American culture. Three others who were introduced to the Delsarte system through Mackaye and Monroe and became leaders in oratorical or actor training were Samuel Silas Curry, Moses True Brown, and Franklin H. Sargent.

Lewis B. Monroe

Monroe (1825–1879) began his professional life as a country schoolteacher and went on to become one of the most influential American educators in oratory and elocution.[3] In 1872 he was appointed founding head of the Boston University School of Oratory, the first such school in an American university and one that would gain great prestige. He remained in this influential post until his death.

Early in his career, Monroe had become familiar with the philosophy of Emanuel Swedenborg (1688–1772). Like Delsarte (see Chapter 6), he was attracted to Swedenborg's doctrine of correspondence between the outward and visible, on the one hand, and the inward and invisible, on the other. For those involved in training for expression, this concept provided a basis for theorizing the relationship between the inner and outer nature of the human being and thus taking both into account in the development of a training methodology. Monroe had expressed his commitment to this concept well before hearing of Delsarte's work. In his 1869 treatise of exercises designed to promote "symmetry of form," "proper position and carriage of the body," "right habits of breathing," "good voice," and "health" (1869: 4–7), Monroe stated that "the Creator's laws are so perfectly balanced, that the highest good of the soul is connected with the highest good of the body" and that "mind and body are mutually dependent" (1–2). While the emphasis in this volume is on voice training, it anticipates much that would later be presented as "Delsartean."

It is not surprising that when Monroe was introduced to the Delsarte system in late 1870, he was immediately receptive and eagerly set out to learn as much about it as possible. He studied with Mackaye, invited Mackaye and other Delsarteans to lecture at the School of Oratory, and incorporated Delsartean theory and practice into his own teaching. Monroe was an enthusiastic advocate of the system for the rest of his life. As a leader in the field of oratory, and as a teacher of subsequent leaders, he ensured its prominence in his profession as well as in the burgeoning physical culture movement to which some of his students were drawn. When he died, the School of Oratory was separated from the university and re-established as a private institution by Robert R. Raymond, a former student of Monroe's, who served as its principal until 1884. To continue Monroe's work at Boston University, a department in oratory was established in its School of All Sciences. Samuel S. Curry, a student of Monroe's, was put in charge, succeeding Monroe as "Snow Professor of Oratory" (Renshaw 306).

William R. Alger

Alger (1822–1905) was a prominent Unitarian minister and the author of several books and articles on a range of subjects including religious matters, Middle Eastern and Asian poetry, the actor Edwin Forrest, and various aspects of Delsartism.[4] He was so enthralled with the Delsarte system that he studied for some years with Mackaye and also traveled to Paris to learn from Delsarte himself. The elder Delsarte's unexpected death prevented that, but Alger worked for some months with Gustave—for good or ill, depending on one's opinion of this son's abilities—and arranged for the transfer of François Delsarte's manuscripts to Mackaye.

In his own Delsarte work, Alger emphasized what he saw as the spiritual side of Delsarte's theory, and he alone of the first three American Delsarteans (he, Mackaye, and Monroe) popularized that aspect. Alger claimed that the Delsarte system was actually religious culture and considered the Delsartean aesthetic gymnastics to be "the basis of a new religious education, destined to perfect the children of men, abolish deformity, sickness, and crime, and redeem the earth" (quoted in Adams 1893). Delsarte's Law of Correspondence and related theories confirmed in Alger his own passionate belief that the physical manifests the spiritual. In his teaching and writings, Alger emphasized those aspects of Delsartism that justified attention to the human body as an expressive instrument. He was active in teaching the Delsarte system and lecturing and writing about it from the early 1870s until his death.

Samuel Silas Curry

With the intention of preparing for the ministry, Curry (1847–1921) entered Boston University to study theology.[5] His education also included work in elocution under Monroe at the School of Oratory, and there, in the early 1870s, he became acquainted with the Delsarte system and Steele Mackaye. Abandoning his theological studies for training in expression, Curry worked intensively and received his master's degree in 1878 and doctorate in 1880.

Curry was an indefatigable student and sought training from many sources in the United States and Europe. The core of his Delsarte study was with Monroe and Mackaye, but, in an 1897 advertisement for his School of Expression, he claimed to have studied with "all the pupils of Delsarte in Paris" (*Werner's Magazine*, vol. 19, n.p.), and elsewhere "with every known pupil of Delsarte" (Curry 1891: 337). Such statements are puzzling, because Mackaye was the only American known to have studied with Delsarte, and there is little record of Delsartean teachers in Paris. Curry might have worked with Giraudet or even Delaumosne, but he mentions neither by name. Among the non-Delsarteans he worked with were Regnier in Paris, Mackaye's original choice of mentor in 1869; Francesco Lamperti (1813–1892), professor of singing at the Milan Conservatory, who reportedly did some Delsarte work with Henrietta and Edmund Russell in the 1880s; Alexander Graham Bell; Alexander Melville Bell; and teachers in England.

As noted above, Curry was appointed Snow Professor of Oratory at Boston University in 1879 and carried on Monroe's work there. In 1888, he organized his own School of Expression with his wife Anna Baright Curry. She had studied under Monroe for four years, been appointed his assistant, and then had opened her own school. The Currys' joint school incorporated a School of Acting that offered the same training as the School of Expression with some additional work relevant to dramatic performance. Under some 40 years of direction by the Currys, their school attracted students from around the country.

Curry developed a theoretical foundation and practical methodology that incorporated elements from the Delsarte and other current systems of expression, oratory, acting, and elocution. He was particularly interested in the psychological aspects of expression and believed that the mind was primary in the act of expression—that mechanical physical

and vocal techniques were, of course, necessary, but that they were in-
effective without the mind and soul being properly engaged. He wrote:

> [W]e find that expression is a product of nature. Every prod-
> uct implies *cause, means,* and *effect*. Expression is the effect of
> rational and emotional activity . . . of the possession of an idea
> by the mind, or of the mind being possessed or dominated by
> an idea or passion. Thus we see at once that the *cause* of ex-
> pression is psychic.
>   The *means* of expression are physical. The thought and the
> emotion depend for revelation upon the body and voice of
> the man. (1891: 207)

Technical training was necessary in his approach, but the actor must
think and feel what he was playing for it to be believable (see also
McTeague 123–25).

While Curry rejected some aspects of the Delsarte system—particularly the Law of Trinity and what he considered an overemphasis on
pantomime—he did incorporate the harmonic gymnastics and other
components into his own curriculum, thereby introducing them to a
broad spectrum of students over the years. In Chapter 18 of his *Province
of Expression*, "The Speculative School," Curry provides an in-depth critique of Delsarte's system and what he considered its distortions in the
United States. Curry wrote 14 books and published numerous articles in
the Werner magazines and in the School of Expression magazine, *Expression*, which he edited and which, of course, promoted his own school.
He was one of the major leaders and thinkers in the field of expression
of his day.

Moses True Brown

Brown (1827–1900) began his professional career in public school
teaching and administration.[6] His interest in elocution was sparked by a
meeting with William Russell, a noted educator and writer who was
promoting elocutionary training in the lower schools (for information on
Russell, see Robb 1954: 187–89). Brown studied with Russell and committed himself to the field of elocution. From 1866 to 1884, he held the
Chair of Oratory at Tufts University in the Boston area. From 1884 to
1894, he was president and owner of the Boston School of Oratory, which
had been separated from Boston University in 1879. He also lectured at
universities and colleges in other locations and was active in professional
elocutionary associations.

Information about Brown's training in the Delsarte system is practically nonexistent. In contrast to Curry, who claimed to have studied with

many Delsarteans on both sides of the Atlantic, Brown's writings include almost nothing about his instructional or written sources. His obituary states that after his appointment at Tufts, Brown had come "under the personal influence" of Monroe ("Moses True Brown" 172); and Brown mentions having first "listened to and witnessed Mr. Mackaye's illustrations of Delsarte," probably in the fall of 1869 (*The Voice* 6 [June 1884]: 91–92). Of course, that date is too early; perhaps he was remembering Mackaye's first presentation of March 1871. One can only assume that Brown's primary knowledge of the Delsarte system must have come originally from Monroe and Mackaye and perhaps occasional articles in *The Voice* and then from the publications that began to be issued in the United States in 1882. He refers to the writings of Delaumosne, Arnaud, and Stebbins in his 1886 book, *The Synthetic Philosophy of Expression*. It is also possible that he had some instruction from Genevieve Stebbins when she taught at Monroe's school and privately in Boston, but his tone when referring to her is sceptical. The only other references to Brown's research into the system are (1) Shawn's claim that Brown had access to the original manuscripts of Delsarte when they were in the hands of Monroe; and (2) a small news item from 1892, when Brown apparently first traveled to Europe. It states that he made "exhaustive studies in both Paris and London of all that pertains to Delsarte" and discovered that the system was taught better in America than in Europe (*Werner's Voice Magazine* 14 [October 1892]: 311). One wonders with whom he made such "exhaustive studies." The only known Delsartean who would have been teaching then was Giraudet in Paris, and Brown seems to have known nothing of him.

However Brown obtained his knowledge of the Delsarte system, beginning in 1882, he appeared regularly on the pages of Werner's magazines as an established Delsartean authority. In addition to articles he wrote and synopses of his lectures, there are news items and advertisements for his lecture series, "New Philosophy of Expression as Formulated and Taught by Delsarte," his summer sessions on the Delsarte system (from 1883 on), and his book (from 1886 on).

All of Brown's writing focuses on the Delsarte system, which he compares with ideas of other current and past thinkers. His sole book, *The Synthetic Philosophy of Expression*, is a philosophical discussion of the Delsarte system as understood by American Delsarteans in the mid-1880s with attention to both general principles and the specific agents of expression—the parts of the body and the voice. As was typical of "serious" writers of his day, Brown refers to numerous (more than 150) authorities to back up his arguments and set his writing in a broad intellectual context. These include scientists, philosophers, writers, and artists. In the Preface he particularly stresses the relevance of the work of Charles Darwin and Paolo Mantegazza, an Italian specialist on expression who had published a book on its relation to physiognomy in 1885. Brown states his intention "to show how the philosophy of these great discoverers [Darwin, Delsarte, and Mantegazza] may be applied to the conscious art forms which every expressive speaker must employ" (1886: vii). He warns that, in contrast to the systematized and fully presented work of the other "great discoverers," knowledge of the Delsarte system is fragmentary (1886: v) and is mainly known as it has filtered through the minds of others such as Delaumosne, Arnaud, Mackaye, and Stebbins. Thus in his detailed critique of the Delsarte system, he often refers to components as "accredited to" Delsarte and questions their validity in comparison with other theory. This is one of the major Delsartean texts of the era.

Franklin H. Sargent

In the 1870s Sargent (?–1924) was a student of Monroe's at the Boston University School of Oratory and was introduced to the Delsarte system at a Mackaye lecture in 1878.[7] After graduation, his first post was teaching elocution and dramatic reading at Harvard. In 1882 Mackaye hired him to train actors for his Madison Square Theatre, and it is at this point that Sargent began daily lessons with Mackaye, work that he considered the most important of his training. In 1884 the two men collaborated in the founding and initial running of the Lyceum Theatre School of Acting. When Mackaye was beset with financial and other problems, Sargent took over and reorganized the school. He renamed it the New York School of Acting in 1885 and then the American Academy of Dramatic Arts in 1892. Under this name it has continued to the present day as a highly respected institution.

Soon after the Lyceum School was founded, Sargent appointed Delsartean rather than traditional acting teachers because he wished to establish that system as the foundation of the training. Looking back on the history of Delsartism in America, Sargent wrote that, although he might criticize some aspects of Delsarte's work, "there is, however, in his instruction the richest vein of precious art-principles that have ever been opened to the world's vision" (Sargent 1890: Part III: 69). In his adaptation of the Delsarte-Mackaye system, Sargent emphasized pantomime and creativity.

Besides his practical work in the training of actors, Sargent wrote an 11-part series of articles, "The Silent Art; A Study of Pantomime and Action," that ran in *Werner's Voice Magazine* from January 1890 to March 1891. After considering pantomime in its theoretical and historical contexts, Sargent devoted sections to mechanism, charm, elements, principles, drama, the platform (where orators performed), and the stage, many of which contain references to the Delsarte system. Sargent built on what Delsarte only suggested—the effect of physical actions on inner states of thought and emotion, a point that would become of great interest in twentieth-century actor training. In contrast to the idea that there is a one-way passage from internal states to external action or utterance, Sargent noted that the influence goes the other way also: the practice of anything with the voice or body will arouse particular feelings and thoughts. As he put it, "The least shading of exterior form or motions incites a corresponding activity of the interior elements of our being." It follows, therefore, that

> the pantomime and elocution teacher is . . . more than a body
> and voice-tuner. He is an educator of the very interior powers
> themselves. He calls up and directs the progress of the natures
> at will, just so far as he is a skilled scientist in his practical
> knowledge of the meaning and value of each agent of ex-
> pression. (1890: Part I: 12)

Thus Sargent shared the characteristic Delsartean belief that training in expression affected the very nature of the student.

American interest in the Delsarte system grew under the careful nurturing of Mackaye, Alger, Monroe, and their followers and attracted the interest of prominent men such as the actor Edwin Forrest, the poet Henry W. Longfellow, political figures, professors, and writers. While both Delsarte and Mackaye situated their theory and practice in the broad context of cultivated life in general, they were mainly involved in the training of professionals in acting, singing, and oratory. It is noteworthy that in this earliest or core phase of Delsartism, the leadership was male as was much of the clientele. Delsarte, Mackaye, and their followers of course had female students as well as males, but the phase of Delsartism closest to Delsarte himself was solidly within the context of a male-controlled professional arena.

The situation changed as two women took what they had learned from Mackaye and others and began to develop the Delsartean material into educational, recreational, and amateur performance activity for women. While they still continued to teach aspiring professionals and would not refuse an occasional male student, both Henrietta Hovey and Genevieve Stebbins used what they had learned to develop the Delsarte system into a training complex within which women (and their female children) could enhance their cultural knowledge, health, and beauty. What they developed became highly appealing to a middle- and upper-class clientele, and Hovey, Stebbins, and their followers were able to earn a substantial part of their income by catering to this female market that they had created. Henrietta Hovey and Genevieve Stebbins were two of the most prominent American Delsarteans to influence both contemporary women's behavior and twentieth-century dance. They, and some of their lesser-known colleagues, will be discussed in the next three chapters.

NOTES

1. Biographical information from Percy Mackaye 1927; Mary Medberry Mackaye; McTeague 1993: 1–43; and materials from the Mackaye Collection at Dartmouth College Library.

2. Steele Mackaye, undated letter to M. M. Mackaye, Delsarte Archive, Louisiana State University, Box 14, Folder 156. In this letter, he asks his wife to develop an article for publication to clarify the Mackaye-Delsarte relationship as well as the question of who had invented harmonic gymnastics. The result was M. M. Mackaye 1892.

3. For information on Monroe, see "Lewis Baxter Monroe"; Thompson 1892a; Renshaw; Wilbor 1887: 254–58.

4. For information on Alger, see Price 1941; Adams 1893b; and listings in the *National Cyclopedia of American Biography*, 6:34–35, and the *Dictionary of American Biography* 1:180–81.

5. For information on Curry, see Robb 1954: 193–97; Curry 1885: 43; McTeague 1993: 121–57; Renshaw 1954; and listing in *National Cyclopedia of American Biography*.

6. Information on Brown from Werner 1889; "Moses True Brown" (obituary); and news items in Werner's magazines.

7. For information on Sargent and the schools, see Hodge 1954; McTeague 1993; McArthur 1984: 100–103.

Chapter 3

Henrietta Hovey: From the Fashionable Salon to the School of Denishawn

The floor of the clubroom of the Coates house was carpeted yesterday afternoon with society ladies.... [After work on voice culture and yawning, Mrs. Russell] introduced her great specialty, and fell down. Then she had the whole class stand up and fall down.... Mrs. Russell says that there is no better gymnastic exercise in the world than falling down. ("Gymnastics for Ladies," *Kansas City Journal* 24 January 1893)

[In 1915] a white haired elderly woman came back stage ... this was the Mrs. Richard Hovey who had been the teacher of Mary Perry King. I began that summer, and ... took private lessons from Mrs. Hovey—as many each week as I could crowd in—and she taught me the true science of François Delsarte, ... and gave me the basis for all my performing, teaching and lecturing career ever since. (Shawn 1974: 12)

Henrietta Hovey has the distinction of having been both the purveyor of titillating cultivation and physical daredeviltry to the socially prominent ladies of her day *and* the serious mentor of Ted Shawn, one of the most important figures in the early development of modern dance. This chapter traces her life and career. I am discussing her before Genevieve Stebbins, not because she was more important, but rather because she was the first American to begin the widespread popularization of the Delsarte system outside the fields of acting and oratory.

Born 6 April 1849 in Cooperstown, New York, as Henrietta Knapp, this renowned American Delsartean had three marriages; thus during her life she was known as Henrietta Crane, then Crane-Russell, Russell, and finally Hovey.[1] Most of her Delsartean teaching was in wealthy society circles where she focused on dress, deportment, and grace, but she initially did some teaching in "art camps" and other arts contexts, and in later life she had a direct influence on the development of American modern dance by working with Shawn; his partner Ruth St. Denis; and their school and company, Denishawn. Hovey taught and lectured up to the time of her death in Pasadena, California, on 16 March 1918.

There is little information known about Henrietta's early life. According to Allan Houston Macdonald, her last husband's biographer, she was a sickly child whose doctor recommended a change from the customary restrictive clothing of the day to loose-fitting garb. This may have been the foundation of her lifelong attention to clothing in relation to both health and aesthetics. The widespread movement for women's clothing reform had begun around the time of her birth and would develop throughout the rest of the century (see, for example, Banner; Ecob; Newton; Potter), and in this endeavor, as in others, Henrietta benefited by aligning herself with a popular cause. By her early twenties she was reportedly designing her own unique costumes and lecturing on dress reform. One reporter claimed that some of her fabrics were designed by New York artists who recognized her as an artist also (Bradshaw 1891: 181). Henrietta's presentational style elicited responses, such as the following:

> Reclining upon a sofa . . . [was] the high priestess of the most aesthetic cults of London, the fair exponent of the Delsartean principles of color, form, and gesture, the concentrated embodiment of the aesthetic ideas of William Morris, Burne-Jones, Rossetti and the other pre-Raphaelite artists of London. Mrs. Russell is a handsome brunette, about medium height, with a willowy physique, and finely cut, intellectual features. She was arrayed in a singular looking gown of ruby velvet, with an inner vest and petticoat of a dull orange-hued silk, the long mediaeval sleeves being of the same stuff. (Bradshaw 1891: 181)

In either the late 1860s or late 1870s, Henrietta bore a child, Howard Kenneth Crane, to her shadowy first husband, Edward B. Crane, whom she had probably met in Boston.[2] She used the name Crane until 1885, although there is no further mention of the husband and little of the son, who was cared for by others. The latter practice became a typical pattern for Henrietta. She bore four children—three of whom survived—but raised none of them. She later wrote: "I never once for one minute neglected one of my boys for 'Fame,' but always for bread—quite a different matter. If I am less than an ideal mother, I am more nearly a good father than most mothers would or could be. . . . I have, moreover, no knack with children" (quoted in Macdonald 152). Henrietta's professional life took priority. Two later children were born before she had married their fathers, and it was of course important to keep their existences hidden to avoid shocking and alienating her respectable clientele. It is interesting to consider that, despite the (at least overt) prudery of nineteenth-century polite society, Henrietta engaged in sexual relationships outside of marriage with no apparent inhibition. In contrast to Isadora Duncan, who gloried in her right to live out her desires (see, for example, Duncan 1927: 254), Henrietta discreetly hid her unconventional behavior.

To improve her speech for public presentations, Henrietta had entered the Boston University School of Oratory sometime after its founding in 1872 and studied there for perhaps as long as two years. From training with Lewis B. Monroe and attendance at Mackaye's lectures, she learned about the Delsarte system—which would subsequently provide her with an identity, a mission, and a livelihood. In a quest for more training, she managed to travel to Paris, probably in 1878, although that may have been the year when her first son was born. There she met Delsarte's widow and perhaps his daughters Marie and Madeleine and studied with Gustave prior to the latter's death in February 1879. How she paid for either her studies in Boston or her Paris trip and how long she worked with Delsarte's son are unanswerable questions. Macdonald writes that Gustave employed Henrietta as his assistant and interpreter for English-speaking students (63), which may or may not be true. In any case, her study in France gave her the credentials to return to the United States and present herself as an authority on the system. As "Mrs. Henrietta Crane" she began to establish herself in the public sphere as a leading Delsartean pundit.

In the summer of 1879, Henrietta gave a three-month series of lectures for a life-drawing class at the National Academy of Design and into the early 1880s she reportedly had teaching engagements at normal schools (teacher-training institutions) in New York and other states (Drew). In December 1881, *The Voice* presented her as a serious Delsarte authority along with the Reverend William R. Alger by publishing interviews with them on "The Delsarte Philosophy" (Alger 1881; Hovey 1881). Both had studied with Gustave, and at this early date, Crane, Mackaye, and Alger were the only three recognized American Delsartean specialists (Monroe had died in 1879 and Stebbins had not yet established herself as a leader in the field). In this interview, Henrietta highly praised Gustave's teaching, suggesting that he may have been "equal or superior to his father"

(Hovey 1881: 176–77). Of course, this was self-serving since she had never studied with François Delsarte.

In 1890 (by which time American Delsartism was a full-blown fad) a severely critical evaluation of Henrietta and Gustave was presented in an anonymous article on the editorial page of *The Voice*. According to this account, when Henrietta went to study with Gustave, he "could speak but little English and [she] could speak but little French; besides he knew very little of his father's method, he having led a wild life and having just returned from a long sojourn out of France" ("False Delsartism"). The unidentified author attributes most of Henrietta's knowledge of the Delsarte system to the lectures of Mackaye; the writings of Delaumosne, Arnaud, and Stebbins; and articles in Werner's magazines. He (or she) critiques Henrietta's presentations as not truly Delsartean. It is impossible to say who might have written this, but the article points to a question that continually arises in relation to Henrietta's credibility and significance as a Delsartean leader. Was she—as characterized by a *New York World* reporter—simply the "shrewdest of clever aesthetes, . . . busily engaged in skimming the cream of the cream" (Pendennis)? Or was she seriously committed to the study, understanding, and teaching of the Delsarte material in its various contexts? Perhaps she was both. Shawn, of course, who met her in her later life, took her very seriously and respected her knowledge, but it is difficult to evaluate her earlier work.

In the summer of 1884, Crane was teaching at an art camp near Detroit (see Case 1885). It was probably there that she became involved with the self-styled artist and poet Edmund Russell, who would become her second husband. A gushing 1886 article in *The Voice* reports that Russell had come to Crane for instruction in the "Delsarte Science and Philosophy of Art, [and] at once fell in love with system—and teacher [and became] wedded to both" ("Delsarte's Art Universal"). The historian Richard A. Meckel presents a more sober account: when the two met in 1884, Edmund already had a reputation as a Delsartean proponent and they joined forces as a lecture team (Meckel 67).[3] Whatever the real story of their meeting, by the fall of 1884 Henrietta and Edmund were lovers, and on 12 July 1885, Sigurd Naourn Russell was born in Des Moines, Iowa. In late 1885 his parents married. Sigurd spent much of his childhood, and received most of his upbringing and education, in France.

After teaching together in New York for a while, the Russells traveled to London in June 1886 to spread the Delsarte gospel there. Despite their own claims (made upon returning to the United States) that they had taken London by storm (Sanburn; Wilbor 1889), it is difficult to verify the nature of their impact. They must have achieved some success in teaching as that would have been their source of income. In an interview published in May 1889, Edmund stated that in London they taught members of the companies of the Drury Lane Theatre, Covent Garden, and the Carl Rosa Opera Company as well as actors and singers from other groups and a number of clergymen and lawyers. He claims that they even had lecture engagements and "a class of five Indian princes" at Cambridge University (Wilbor 1889). Henrietta's address book (which had been copied in 1900 from an earlier one) includes almost 150 people with English (mostly London) addresses and a list of 24 "East Indians."[4] In statements such as Edmund's and in the address book, there is a heavy sprinkling of prestigious folk—from the aristocracy, politics, the arts, and literature. The latter two categories include figures such as Felix Moscheles, Robert Browning, Walter Crane, Holman Hunt, and Oscar Wilde.

There was one publication from this era that almost certainly would have provided detailed information about the Russells' activities in England. This is *The Elocutionist*, published in London from 1882 to 1891, with coverage similar to that of Werner's magazines in the United States. In its April 1886 issue, there is an announcement that the Russells would be coming to London to teach Delsartism. Unfortunately, most of the British Library's holdings of this periodical were destroyed during World War II, and there have been no issues found later than April 1886.

With a few exceptions, little was written about the Russells or the Delsarte system in the mainstream London press. The first two of their presentations did get some coverage. In late June they gave a lecture at the studio of the portrait painter Felix Moscheles (1833–1917), whom one or both had met during his mid-1880s stay in the United States (Wilbor 1889). This introduction elicited praise for Henrietta's "extraordinary gracefulness as she showed how different feelings and emotions were expressed on the Delsartean principle," and the prediction that "the cult [of Delsartism] seems certainly to have in it the elements of a London success" ("Occasional Notes" 29 June 1886). A more formal presentation—"The Harmony and Expression of Motion" at the Drury Lane Theatre, 31 July 1886, received a mixed review:

> "Beautiful Edmund Russell" is among us, but Mr. Oscar Wilde has nothing to fear. It is only in the reflected light of Mrs. Russell that this gentleman appears attractive at all. He is a species of propriety padding, and his share [in the program] . . . may be dismissed with that remark. Mrs. Russell is a much more serious person. She represents that large section of Americans who really study elocution—or try to—and gesture and the general philosophy of physical expression. ("Occasional Notes" 2 August 1886)

The audience was reportedly small on this occasion ("Harmony and Expression of Motion").

After these initial presentations in 1886, there is little in print about the Russells' activities until 1888. In fact, from September 1886 until April 1888, there is no hint at all of their whereabouts except for Edmund's mention in a May 1889 article that they had spent the summer of 1887 in Italy with the Milan opera teacher Francesco Lamperti, teaching Delsartism to his pupils (Wilbor 1889).

In the spring of 1888, the Russells embarked on what they should have realized was a foolhardy venture: they presented themselves as actors. In two matinees at London's Princess Theatre, they attempted to show the value of the Delsarte system for the actor through their own performance—and the reviews were scathing. Of Henrietta in the title role of Racine's *Phèdre* (translated by a Dr. A. W. Momerie and presented on 16 April), the critic for *The Era* wrote:

> If what we saw and heard . . . is to be regarded as the outcome of the Delsartean method . . . we may express the hope that the English stage may long be spared its general adoption. An exhibition more ridiculous than that presented on this occasion, and a greater travesty of a great author, has seldom, if ever, come under our observation. . . . The *raison d'être* of the performance was, of course, to give Mrs. Russell an opportunity of exploiting herself as a tragic actress. . . . [H]er tragedy was very comical . . . she was altogether out of her element. (" 'Phèdre' in Fun")

On 20 April, Edmund in *Ion* (by T. N. Talfourd; first produced 1836, Covent Garden) fared even worse. The same critic wrote of his "monotonous delivery . . . reminding one . . . of the delivery of a soporific sermon by a High Church curate. His favorite "pose" was to stand with his right arm extended as if he were sitting for a sculptor, or were going to catch a fly" (" 'Phèdre' in Fun"). However, the critic considered the overall production of *Ion* better than that of *Phèdre*.

The consensus among all who reviewed these productions (see also *The Dramatic Review* (London) (28 April 1888: 124–25); and *The Society Herald* (London) (23 April 1888: 19) was that they would discourage rather than encourage anyone from taking an interest in Delsarte training for the theater. Reportedly Henrietta did not have enough theatrical knowledge even to project her voice or apply appropriate make-up, and both she and Edmund were criticized for their physical work, despite the fact that this was a fundamental aspect of the Delsarte system. One wonders at the Russells' naïveté in thinking they could succeed in a field in which neither had training or experience. While they may have (as they claimed) lectured on the Delsarte system to theater groups and worked some with actors on its principles, there is no evidence that either had done any serious study or work in the actor's art, theater direction, or technical theater, all of which would be necessary to mount a successful production.

From May 1888 to April 1889, there is again no record of the Russells. In the spring of 1889, Edmund returned to the United States and attempted to promote a society of Delsarteans with Mackaye at the head ("A Plea for Organization"). Nothing came of it. In June 1889 he began advertising in *Werner's Voice Magazine* as a Delsarte teacher. Meanwhile, Henrietta stayed behind in Europe, purportedly to plan a teaching trip to Sweden (Wilbor 1889) that probably never took place. It seems that the Russells had separated by this time. Individually each tried to capitalize on the growing American interest in Delsartism and to cultivate press coverage with news of his or her London successes, almost as if the other did not exist.

It is difficult to corroborate the Russells' statements about their activities and impact in England. A close examination of memoirs, autobiographies, and biographies of some of the famous folk they claim to have impressed turned up no mention of the Delsarte system or the Russells. What seems likely is that they did have an active teaching stint in London—some of it in high society—and did meet at least some of the well-known figures whose names they later cited to impress prospective American students. However, there is no evidence that any of the rich and famous found the Russells or the Delsarte system of major importance in their lives.

By October 1889, both Russells were permanently back in the United States, and they independently pursued careers as Delsartean gurus newly returned from triumphs abroad. Henrietta engaged a manager, Major J. B. Pond, to help her develop her own following. She also, of course, advertised in *Werner's*, billing herself as Henrietta (Crane) Russell, Henrietta Russell, or Mrs. Edmund Russell until her marriage to Hovey. Such designations helped create something of a smoke screen around the actual relationship between Edmund and Henrietta, both professionally and personally. Henrietta's efforts to re-establish her identity as a Delsartean specialist in her own right were sometimes undermined in the press when she was identified as "wife of the Delsartean Apostle" as if she were the follower of her husband. This impression was fostered by Edmund at every opportunity and would have seemed credible to a society that saw men as leaders and women as followers. The 1890 *Delsartean Scrapbook* reinforced such confusion. It featured the two of them as "the high priest and priestess of Delsarte" as if they were still a team, but included two to three times more coverage of Edmund than of Henrietta. Presenting them as continuing collaborators was good for selling the book and for their individual exploitation of the Delsarte craze, which would reach its peak in the 1890s, but one wonders how much say Henrietta had in the content and focus of this volume. Their disciples were not unaware of their competition. One item that was purportedly printed in Dallas and Grand Rapids newspapers as well as in Chicago noted that "the ladies that go in for the Delsarte school of expression divide their adoration with more or less impartiality between Mr. and Mrs. Edmund Russell" (*Chicago Times* 22 February 1890).

Edmund appeared less and less in the literature on Delsartism, but at least through the end of the century, he was still presenting himself as an authority on it. As Suzanne Shelton, Ruth St. Denis' biographer, has expressed it, "Russell was an odd one, an aesthete who affected flowing oriental robes and surrounded himself with coveys of young men. He fancied himself a high priest of the social set, offering lessons in deportment and Delsartean aesthetics" (1981: 49). He was mocked in a *Werner's Magazine* editorial in 1899 as a "pink tea elocutionist," a term coined for men "who devote themselves to, and whose livelihood comes from, society women" and who are used as a kind of variety entertainment for their guests (22, no. 6 [February 1899]: 465, 467).

We might ask why Henrietta was not also dubbed "pink tea." Was she somehow more convincing in her claims of furthering both lofty and practical goals, or more skillful at self-promotion? Or was it because she was a woman, and this type of pandering to society seemed more appropriate for the distaff side? An 1889–1890 brochure with laudatory press clippings and testimonials presented Henrietta as a Delsartean authority on the fine arts as well as on cultivated behavior and self-presentation. She offered herself for lectures on "The Teachings of Delsarte (Illustrated by Gesture and Action)," "Expression in Oratory, Acting, Painting and Sculpture," "Grace of Motion—Walking, Bowing, and Dancing," "Artistic Dress," and "American Art—Present and Future." The review of a session probably given in late 1889 stresses the practical intent of her teaching:

> If every woman who attended the last of Mrs. Edmund Russell's course of lectures at Hardman Hall . . . doesn't find her carriage somewhat improved thereby it will be a clear case of age, infirmity or constitutional awkwardness and not the fault of that eminently graceful exponent of Delsarte's methods. (*New York World* clipping in Hovey Papers, n.d.)

Henrietta's offerings were somewhat revised in an advertisement for a series of eight lectures to be given at Hardman Hall in New York City during March and April of 1890. That list omitted any mention of oratory, acting, and dancing and included a session titled "How to Spend Money." This is interesting in light of the fact that much of Henrietta's life was spent scraping by on much less than her needs and tastes required.

Apparently, Major Pond's promotion worked as Henrietta was engaged for lectures not only in New York City, but also in Washington, D.C., Philadelphia, and other locations during the winter and spring of 1889–1890. News of her activities and opinions traveled even further afield with press items being reprinted as far away as Chicago, Dallas, Milwaukee, and Grand Rapids, Michigan. Of course Delsartism was already becoming popular across the country and people were interested in news of it and of this intriguing and socially prestigious spokeswoman.

The Pond brochure reproduced what seems to have been a conscious and misguided attempt by Henrietta to embellish her credibility as a Delsarte authority. Instead of specifying that she had worked with Gustave (which the 1881 interview made clear), she apparently gave misleading information in press interviews. For example, a passage attributed to the *Iowa Tribune* states: "For several years a pupil and assistant of Delsarte, she holds in trust a precious heritage of the thought and words of a man who spoke more than he wrote." This would lead one to believe that she had studied with the elder rather than the younger Delsarte. It is puzzling that she did not realize that such dishonesty would discredit her in the eyes of anyone who knew the truth about her training.[5]

By the 1890–1891 season, Henrietta was developing her fashionable clientele in a number of locations. A particularly important venue for her was Newport, Rhode Island, which drew a wealthy and prestigious crowd in the summer. The women of families such as the Vanderbilts, Whitneys, and Astors flocked to Henrietta's lessons (held in one of their homes) to work on moving gracefully, wearing jewels and clothing that were aesthetically complementary, and, of course, the notorious and apparently highly enjoyable falling. Peggy Pendennis reported in the *New York World*:

> Newport has gone daft over Delsarte. . . . Henrietta . . . came, saw and conquered. Came to be not only listened to but received socially. . . . The choicest cullings from the smart set meet twice a week to writhe, wriggle, bend and sway; to relax and decompose . . . [to] form spiral curves and make corkscrews of themselves, . . . not only does Mrs. Russell teach these ladies how to bow, smile, walk and sit down, but how to fall gracefully and lie, a limp little mass of tangled lace and drapery, upon the floor.

Such effusions, however, still did not earn her Werner's "pink tea" designation. From reports such as this, frivolous as they were, it seems that

Henrietta was teaching physical exercises similar to those of Genevieve Stebbins (see Chapter 8), which is not surprising. Even though she began in the Delsarte business before Stebbins had published anything, Henrietta's physical work could easily have been based on the latter's *Delsarte System of Expression* as well as what she had gotten from the Mackaye lectures years before.

Sometime in the fall or winter of 1889, Henrietta had met the young poet Richard Hovey, who, along with his friend Bliss Carman, was interested in the Delsarte system. Eventually a relationship developed between them, although Henrietta was at the time still married to Edmund. They became lovers and on 9 February 1892 their son Julian (originally named Radegund) was born in Tours, France, where he was left in the care of a nurse. Henrietta's press coverage during this period claimed that she was abroad spreading Delsartism to eager patrons. On 17 January 1894, Henrietta and Hovey were married in Boston.

Until the late 1890s, Henrietta taught and lectured on the Delsarte system in various locations in the United States and on trips with Hovey to London, France, and Nova Scotia (see Macdonald 72–188 for details of these travels). She received broad press coverage and the clippings she assiduously collected document her focus on the enhancement of her clients' everyday lives through instruction on aesthetics, expression, and physical grace. Her success reflected both the increasing popularity of Delsartism across the United States and her status as the darling of high society. Unfortunately, there is little coverage of what, if any, teaching she may have done in a more serious context.

A typical newspaper account from 1892 (and one more sober than the one quoted above) praises her as a "prominent leader in [the] graceful and artistic study" of "the harmonious development of woman," and tells of her success in teaching the "Delsartean system of expression and development" in "high social and fashionable circles." It describes her approach as follows:

> Her creed is one of newer and stronger life. She presents for attainment the best that a man or woman can be: symmetrical physical development, following the laws which govern motion and emotion, physiology and psychology in one; the relief from nervous tension, the correspondence of action and repose; the use of each power with freedom yet without fatigue; how to breathe, how to walk, how to sit, how to work, how to rest—in short, the training of personality to its best. (unidentified clipping, 5 March 1892)

Again, the similarity to what Stebbins taught is striking.

As her professional life developed, Henrietta added to her teaching repertoire. In a brochure from around 1894, Henrietta's offerings take up two pages and include the following single lectures and series: "What is Delsartism?"; "The Personal Arts" (with 11 sessions on gesture, grace, acting, oratory, ritual and etiquette, walking, bowing, poise, breathing, declamation in singing, and the art of speech); "Delsarte and Poetry" (three sessions, perhaps in collaboration with Hovey); "Modern Movements in Painting and Decoration"; "Attitude and Expression in Painting and Sculpture"; "Architecture"; "The Decorative Arts" (five sessions on the home, dress, jewels, and the hair); "The Use and Abuse of Delsarte Charts" (designated as only for Delsarteans); and finally, "François and Gustave Delsarte." She also announced her willingness to give private lessons in most of the subjects listed above and readings of her husband's poetry.

Henrietta was clearly committed to a broad view of expression, either from her own inclinations or because it was profitable. The phrase "jack-of-all-trades" comes to mind, but, of course, the source of her Delsartean bag of tricks had himself seen his theories as universal and applicable to all aspects of life. One can imagine that Henrietta's society clientele must have been very impressed with her ability to span such a range of subjects and perhaps saw her as somewhat of a role model. She had public visibility and a kind of agency, albeit in a female world. She provided her highly placed "pupils" with an attractive amusement that had the patina of serious cultural endeavor. She was provocative enough to be interesting, but always within the bounds (as far as her clientele knew) of proper middle-class behavioral norms.

Henrietta's reputation continued to grow nationally. In addition to teaching and lecturing engagements in various places, she had published her book *Yawning* (1891), which received press notices across the country from New England to California. In 1893 Henrietta was invited to be one of the speakers at the World's Congress of Representative Women, which was associated with the World's Columbian Exposition in Chicago. She gave a 30-minute presentation as part of a session on dress. This invitation also increased her visibility and prestige.

In May 1894, the Hoveys went to England for an extended stay. Richard was writing while Henrietta continued her Delsarte work. On this visit she received flattering press notices—one claiming that she had been "pupil and assistant teacher for over fifteen years of that great master, Delsarte" and noting the prestigious venues where she had taught in the United States and England (*The Ludgate Illustrated Magazine* September 1894). The Hoveys were soon the center of a social whirl of artists and writers—but they were also suffering from an extreme lack of money (Macdonald 153–55). In mid-1895, they moved to France to be reunited with their son, who was now over three years old. They were even more poverty-stricken in Paris than they had been in London, barely scraping by on the occasional royalty, a loan from someone, small fees that Henrietta could earn lecturing on Delsarte (she could find no private pupils), or other bits of money that might come their way (Macdonald 164–67, 181). In March 1896, they finally managed the return passage home with their son and his nurse in tow.

Back in the United States, Henrietta attempted to rekindle interest in her Delsarte teaching and did give some lectures, but the Delsarte "craze" had waned in her absence and her engagements were few and far between as the decade was coming to an end. Then, on 24 February 1900, Richard unexpectedly died after a minor operation (Macdonald 227–28). Henrietta remained in New York for some years editing and promoting the publication of Hovey's poetry, surely a labor of love, but also the only potential source of income that would have been available for her and the support of her sons. There is no record during these years of her teaching or being otherwise involved in any Delsarte work.

From about 1904 until 1907 or so Henrietta was active, along with Edmund Russell, as one of the founders of a socialist-leaning theatre group called the Progressive Stage Society, a nonprofit organization for the presentation of noncommercial experimental dramas.[6] Financed by small donations from a large number of members, it presented works that presumably would have no market on the commercial stage: socialist plays, Ibsen's *Enemy of the People*, and a performance of *Sakuntala* featuring Edmund Russell and Ruth St. Denis.

Sometime in the fall of 1909, Henrietta moved to the Los Angeles area where she again presented herself as a teacher of Delsartism and once more became well known in society circles. By this time, she was also an ardent supporter of women's suffrage and spoke forcefully and publicly in its favor (see, for example, *Los Angeles Express* 21 January 1911). She claimed to have developed an interest in women's issues as early as 1868. She had been working then as a night-school teacher in an unnamed factory town when she was supplanted by a less successful male teacher who was paid much more (*Los Angeles Express* 3 November 1909). In 1911, she related that after moving to Boston (in the late 1860s or early 1870s), she had come into contact with the women's suffrage movement and learned that "there was a relation between disenfranchisement and financial indignity" (*Los Angeles Express* 21 January 1911). Of course, by 1909, it was now a popular position and helped rather than hindered her status as a newsworthy society figure. There is no evidence of political involvement in her press coverage and statements of the 1880s and 1890s.

It is difficult to reach any conclusions about the exact nature of Hovey's teaching and thus its influence. In contrast to Stebbins, whose writings give a clear and extensive picture of both her theory and her teaching methods and materials, Hovey's record offers very little of substance. There are only society page descriptions of classes she taught in the 1890s, some of which have been quoted above, and the book *Yawning* which she published in 1891. The articles describing her classes are usually in a light, sometimes mocking, vein, and the book is no more than an inspirational tract on the yawn as "nature's gymnastic" with frequent references to Delsarte. It elicited a fair amount of mockery just for its title. Hovey had projected a multivolume work on the Delsarte system of which *Yawning* was to be the first. A very long typewritten draft of other projected sections of this opus is in the Ted Shawn archive at the Dance Collection of the New York Public Library at Lincoln Center, and looks much more substantial than *Yawning*, but neither sheds much light on the inner workings of Hovey's mind or on her actual teaching principles and practices. The woman herself and what she imparted are elusive.

Henrietta, as did other Delsarteans, offered self-improvement based on the concept of mind-body correspondence. The goal was to instill art in all aspects of life and thereby nurture better human beings, to train them to be the "best" that they could be. One is reminded of the statements by both Delsarte and Mackaye that place the Delsarte approach in the grand context of human development rather than limiting it to professional training, but where Delsarte and Mackaye actually focused on the professional in their teachings, Henrietta and others spent much of their time training students for "life" rather than for a career. Without the connection with Shawn, Hovey could probably be dismissed as just one more of the purveyors of American Delsartism in her era. Shawn, however, clearly valued greatly what he had learned from her. That, along with his early exposure to American Delsartean ideas from Bliss Carman and Mary Perry King, stimulated him to research in depth the Delsarte system and everything that had been written about it. He then integrated what he had learned into his own theoretical and aesthetic principles of the art of dance. Through Shawn and Denishawn, Delsartean principles and practical work extended into the nascent modern dance.

Hovey's whole life raises questions. Was she just a clever operator who used what worked to gain a living and renown and to engage in whatever gave her pleasure? Or was she a serious investigator into the principles of physical culture and expression who had something substantial to offer? In her heyday, Hovey was a beautiful, exotic creature who brought an attractive message of self-improvement and cultivation to ladies with the leisure and money to enjoy the "finer things of life." In her maturity, she spent considerable efforts editing her husband's poetry after his death, and apparently was involved in teaching until the end of her life. What a pity that she has divulged so little of what was really important to her. In contrast, the subject of the next chapter was a prolific writer who left a rich and fascinating record of her thinking, her aesthetic theory, her pedagogical goals and practice, and her approach to performance.

NOTES

1. Biographical information from Macdonald 1957; Meckel 1989; *Who's Who in America* (from 1899–1900 until more than 20 years after her death); Henrietta Hovey clippings and other material in the Richard Hovey Papers, Dartmouth College Library; articles and news items in Werner's magazines and other periodicals.

2. On the last page of her 1900 notebook: "Business and Historical Information" (in the Richard Hovey Papers, Dartmouth College Library), Henrietta wrote that Harold Kenneth Crane was born on Easter Sunday, April 21. Easter fell on April 21 in 1867 and 1878. In 1867 Henrietta would have been 18 and in 1878, 29, and involved in her studies in Boston or her travel to France. Since she used the name Crane until 1885, it may be that 1878 was the year this son was born.

3. Macdonald (63) suggests the same, but the only advertisement and news item of Edmund as a Delsarte teacher prior to his marriage to Henrietta were in *The Voice*, January 1885. In that ad, he identifies himself as a pupil of Henrietta Crane.

4. On the first page of this address book, which is in the Hovey Collection at Dartmouth, Henrietta writes that Richard had copied the addresses in it and that "it was the last book in which I had the addresses of my friends separate from his." While some of the names from England may have been people she met in the 1890s when she was there with Hovey, many of them can be verified as dating from her 1886–1889 visit with Russell.

5. Apparently she temporarily did, for around 1894 a new promotional brochure appeared (without reference to Major Pond) that identified her as "pupil and formerly assistant of Gustave Delsarte" and listed, with what seems to be careful accuracy, the locations and recipients of her teaching. However, later statements to the press went back to suggesting that her study had been with François Delsarte.

6. For Progressive Stage Society see Shelton 1981: 49–50; and clippings in the Hovey Collection.

Chapter 4

Genevieve Stebbins:
Teacher and Artist

> At Wellesley, Mrs. Stebbins appeared . . . picturesquely gowned in a
> soft clinging white silk with a Roman sash, the Oriental effect being
> further added by a little zouave jacket in gay colors. She is gifted
> with an expressive, mobile face and a resonant, flexible voice. (N. A.
> 1893: 445)

> I come, my friends, to inaugurate with you, I hope, a crusade of
> health and beauty. . . . I wish to talk to you of the new education. . . .
> [T]he education of the mind and the body at once. (Stebbins quoted
> in "Delsarte Matinee" 149).

Of the many American exponents of the Delsarte system in the late nineteenth century, Genevieve Stebbins has been the most influential due to
both her professional activity and her numerous publications. She investigated, adapted, and further developed the theoretical and practical
work on expression that had originated with Delsarte and been introduced into the United States by Steele Mackaye. Active from the 1870s
through the early twentieth century, her influence spread not only across
the United States, but also to Europe. This chapter covers her life, training, and professional work.

There is little information on Stebbins' early life.[1] She was born 7
March 1857 in San Francisco. Her father, James Cole Stebbins (d. 1889),
from Oneida, New York, was a successful land lawyer in San Francisco.

Her mother, Henrietta Smith Stebbins, the daughter of an Amherst College professor, died in 1859, most probably at the birth of their second child, Lilly Henrietta (b. 16 April 1859). James apparently remarried, to a woman named Adella Randall who may have been responsible for raising the two girls. There is also evidence that Henrietta's older sister, Louise Amelia Knapp Smith Clappe (1819–1906), noted writer of *The Shirley Letters*, was close to the girls and may even have functioned as mother to them. At some point James depleted the family resources through gold mine speculation, but their economic situation still must have been fairly strong to support Genevieve during her years of educational and professional preparation.

Stebbins' interest in performance and expression began to develop early in her life. As a child she reportedly performed pantomimes, songs, dances, and statue poses, at private gatherings and even in public. She received praise for her efforts from admiring relatives and family friends. Given her subsequent intellectual interests and writing abilities, it seems likely that she received a good academic education as well as encouragement of her artistic leanings. Her intellectual development may have owed a great deal to the influence of her aunt Louise.

In 1875, when she was 18, Stebbins traveled to New York City to pursue an acting career. Such a move was not common for a nineteenth-century middle-class girl. While the long-standing prejudice against the theater and its practitioners was lessening in the latter part of the century, it had by no means disappeared (Johnson 1984). Either Stebbins' family was particularly liberal or she went without their knowing what she had in mind. One account says that a friend had invited her to New York to help her find a wealthy husband (Wilbor 1887: 289–90). Clearly Stebbins had other plans in mind.

Stebbins initially studied with the famous actress Rose Eytinge (1835–1911) at the Union Square Theatre and then apparently toured with her as leading juvenile actress. Stebbins' New York City debut was probably 19 February 1877, when she played Violet in *Our Boys* at the New Broadway Theatre (Odell 10:218). A short notice in the *New York Tribune* describes her as "pretty, vivacious, pleasing, and promising" ("Dramatic Notes" 27 February 1877).

Stebbins may have met Steele Mackaye through Rose Eytinge, who had starred in Mackaye's production of *Rose Michel* at the Union Square Theatre during the 1875–1876 season (Odell 10:21–22). In any case, she began to work with Mackaye in late 1876 or early 1877—or, perhaps, with his assistant, Ida Simpson-Serven. A 1902 biographical sketch states that Mackaye had "persuaded her to retire from the stage and study the famous Delsarte system with him for two years, promising her the lead part in a play which he was writing at the time" ("Equipment of the Faculty" 224). This is apparently what she did since she is not listed in any productions between *Our Boys* and her starring role in Mackaye's revival of his *Aftermath; or Won at Last* at the Madison Square Theatre, 23 April–20 May 1879 (Odell 10:652).[2] After this, Stebbins also appeared in a number of other plays including *Hamlet* in 1880 (Odell 11:270), *The Lights o'London* in 1884 (Odell 12:267, 360), *The Merchant of Venice* in 1885 (Odell 12:542), and *Hazel Kirke* in 1885 (Odell 12:562).

In her Delsarte work with Mackaye, Stebbins was an enthusiastic and apt pupil. After a year of study he invited her to demonstrate for his lectures at the Boston University School of Oratory and eventually had her teaching there in his place. In March 1878, Mackaye arranged with Lewis B. Monroe for Stebbins to be admitted to a course of vocal training in the school.[3] Her instructor was Mary S. Thompson with whom Stebbins would collaborate over the next 14 years.

While Stebbins had resumed her acting career, she was at the same time establishing herself as a specialist in the Delsarte system. After completing her vocal studies with Thompson, the two women opened a school together in Boston. Then they resettled in New York and continued their partnership. This included teaching at the same location until the fall of 1892 and giving joint Delsarte programs.

At first, Mackaye was very supportive of Stebbins' independent teaching. In the fall of 1879, she still fully acknowledged that what she knew about the Delsarte system was his material and asked his permission to use it. On 22 September 1879, he answered:

> In reply to your note requesting permission to apply my system of dramatic training [note: he identifies it as *his*] to the instruction of your own pupils, I am glad to assure you that it gives me great pleasure to grant that permission, and to be able to say sincerely that you are thoroughly competent to put that system to good use. You are the only one of my pupils now living whom I can conscientiously recommend or gladly authorize to teach what I teach myself.[4]

As late as 1885, in the introduction to *Delsarte System of Expression*, Stebbins wrote positively of Mackaye (see 1902: 77). However, that relationship of cordiality and mutual respect was to change dramatically during the following few years as Stebbins assumed independence as a Delsarte authority, and as Mackaye saw what he had introduced into the United States taken over by others. Steele and Percy Mackaye railed against those who had been teaching and publishing material the Mackayes considered stolen from Steele (see P. Mackaye 2:269–70). On her side, Stebbins began to downplay what she had learned from Mackaye, even disparaging his character as well as his teachings (see, for example, Stebbins 1893: 58n, 79; Stebbins 1902: 395–96).[5]

In March 1880, Stebbins and Thompson first presented a program of public readings that, by the late 1880s, had developed into an annual "Delsarte Matinee," a kind of variety show that included forms such as statue posing, pantomime, drills, and even dances as well as recitations. Such performances, besides being a source of revenue, promoted the system and its teachings, demonstrated its value to potential students, and entertained the middle- and upper-class ladies who had the time, money, and inclination for self-improvement and cultural activities. In the early 1880s, few people outside the fields of acting and oratory knew about Delsarte's work, and there was as yet no text available in the United States. The Stebbins-Thompson performances helped to popularize the peculiarly American adaptation of the Delsarte system.

In 1881 Stebbins traveled to Europe to investigate the Delsarte system further and write a book on it, a project suggested to her by the publisher Edgar S. Werner (Thompson 1892c: 61), who specialized in literature on elocution, expression, and music. One wonders, at this relatively early date, what evidence Werner had that the Delsarte material was going to elicit enough interest to warrant a second book—he already had the English translation of Delaumosne in process. And what gave him confidence that Stebbins could accomplish the task? As yet, she had published nothing and had barely started to present her Delsarte work on stage. Of the still small group of American Delsarteans she apparently seemed to be the most qualified person, except for Mackaye, whose theatre work never left him time for such a project. Apparently, Werner never considered Alger or Hovey, perhaps because their main training had been with Gustave and they were not professionals in acting or oratory. Reasons for choosing Stebbins over the others may have included the following: she was in a direct line from François Delsarte through Mackaye and had studied intensively with the latter; she was apparently fluent in French; and she had a professional orientation. As it turned out, there would be a market for many books on the Delsarte system, and Stebbins would become the most significant figure in the field and the most prolific and articulate of the Delsartean writers.

In Paris, through his French publisher, Stebbins tracked down the Abbé Delaumosne whose treatise was just then being translated for Werner's English edition and discussed the Delsarte system with him (Stebbins 1902: 73–75). It would not have been impossible for her also to have met Angélique Arnaud and Alfred Giraudet, but there is no indication that she did—and she would surely have mentioned such meetings to promote her own credibility in the field. Regarding the Delsarte family, Gustave had died two years before her visit, and there is surprisingly no record of a meeting with other family members on this first trip. One would have expected her to start with them.

Years later, Stebbins wrote that during this visit to Europe she spent time in the classical collections of museums investigating the validity of Delsarte's theories:

> When I learned that Delsarte had devoted many years to the study of antique statuary, in order to discover the lost principles of classic art, I instantly became impressed with the desire and determination to study the statues also. I was the first Delsartian [*sic*] to do this on the line of artistic investigation. I was young and enthusiastic, filled to overflowing with the ideal possibilities of the Delsarte System. I had just completed two years' study with Steele Mackaye, and the zeal which animated him becoming contagious, produced the same spirit in myself. London, Florence, Rome and Paris became rich fields of my study. I spent months studying the collections of the antique in the galleries of the Louvre, making notes, checking off every law and principle of Delsarte's opposition, sequence, and poise, and trying for one whole year to find a really artistic contradiction to his general formulation, but in vain. (1902: 445–46).

In addition to validating what she had learned of Delsarte's system, this trip must have confirmed for her what was a prevailing enthusiasm of her day—an ardent belief in the timeless perfection of classical art. The great effort and thoroughness she claimed to have applied in her research on this trip would appear to be a characteristic approach to learning that persisted throughout her life.

While in Paris, Stebbins studied acting under François-Joseph Regnier—Mackaye's original choice of mentor—and reported that she gained much from his lessons on "dynamic nerve-energy in the voice, and his many artistic suggestions" (1893: vi). Regnier wrote her a letter, dated 13 June 1882, in which he praised her dramatic qualities and her passion for work and declared that she possessed the true temperament of an artist (reprinted in Stebbins 1888: 109). In the New York School of Expression's first prospectus, Stebbins claimed to have studied in Paris and elsewhere with a number of other notable teachers (*New York School of Expression* 1893: 30).

Stebbins' activities in 1882 and 1883 remain a mystery. Perhaps her study in Europe extended well into 1882, and it may be assumed that either there, or upon returning to the United States, she spent some time writing *Delsarte System of Expression*, which appeared in 1885. From the spring of 1884 through the spring of 1885, Stebbins returned to the professional stage to play at least three roles. A biographical note from 1902 states that in 1885 she "left the theatrical profession and published her first book" and that "its immediate success decided her to become a lecturer and a teacher" ("Equipment of Our Faculty" 224).

What factors led Stebbins to abandon her career in the theatre? Was it mainly because her work with the Delsarte system was becoming more and more of a consuming interest? Or, was she motivated by a realistic perception of her own limited potential as an actress and her stronger abilities as a teacher and writer? In a discussion of John Ruskin's concept of the "divine instinct" as it operates in the artist, Stebbins writes that "my best results have been attained when I, a passive subject, obeyed an inner inspiration coming from whence I know not and urging me on to results I had not aimed at. This, in my own modest efforts, has been my experience: how much more must it be the experience of great artists!" (1902: 337).[6] Was she simply being disingenuous here, or did this reflect her realization that she was not, first and foremost, an artist?

By 1885, Stebbins had completed her basic training in the Delsarte-Mackaye system and published its core ideas and exercises in a form probably very close to what she had learned from her studies with Mackaye and the books of Delaumosne and Arnaud. From 1885 until her retirement in 1907, she devoted herself to teaching, demonstrating (in Delsartean performances), and writing about the theory and practice that she continued to develop on the basis of both her Delsartean training and other studies. Besides *Delsarte System of Expression* (which went through six editions between 1885 and 1902), frequent articles for Werner's publications, and other miscellaneous writings, Stebbins completed three additional important books on physical culture and expression: *Society Gymnastics and Voice Culture* (1888), *Dynamic Breathing and Harmonic Gymnastics* (1893), and *The Genevieve Stebbins System of Physical Training* (1898, 1913). Her writings established her reputation and authority in the field during her own day, and leave a concrete record for us to examine today. They demonstrate both her own individual beliefs and pedagogy and much of the prevailing theory and practice of that time.

From the mid-1880s until the early 1890s, advertisements and news items in Werner's magazines show that Stebbins and Mary S. Thompson, her colleague from the Boston University School of Oratory, taught at the same location in New York City and collaborated on annual Delsarte matinees at Madison Square Theatre (which was no longer under Mackaye's control). In 1886 Stebbins returned to Paris, this time purportedly to read her newly published *Delsarte System of Expression* to Mme. Delsarte for her approval. Perhaps Stebbins was hoping for a public statement of endorsement. Thompson has written that Mme. Delsarte was so impressed with the work that she gave Stebbins the remaining manuscripts of her late husband (1892c: 61). This would have been part of the collection that Mackaye thought he was purchasing after Delsarte died (P. Mackaye 2: Appendix xl, 136n). After her return from Paris, Stebbins continued teaching classes for private pupils, society gatherings, and educational institutions in New York and elsewhere. The latter included regular courses at fashionable girls' schools as well as short-term visits to women's programs in colleges and universities.

By at least 20 March 1888, Stebbins had married Joseph A. Thompson, an attorney and most likely the brother or another relative of Mary Thompson. Nothing is known about him. The marriage apparently ended by October 1892, and its demise seems to be related to a concurrent break in the collaboration of Stebbins with Mary Thompson. Their joint teaching advertisements were also discontinued in October 1892, but the last Delsarte matinee they presented together took place 25 April 1893 (*Werner's Magazine* 15 [May]: 186), during the same month that Stebbins remarried.

Stebbins' second husband, Norman Astley (b. England, 19 April 1853), is listed in *The Stebbins Genealogy* as a journalist (Greenlee and Greenlee 1904: 1099). Another source reports that he had been a captain in the British army and had worked as a surveyor (The Church of Light). Astley seems to have had some interest and background in theater as well and collaborated with Stebbins in the New York School of Expression. In the school's first prospectus Astley is listed as the head of its department of dramatic criticism with qualifications of "natural ability, training and foreign travel" (14). An article on the school states that he taught a course on "stage technique and grouping for tableaux vivants" and that he was the author of many of Stebbins' pantomimes ("The New York School of Expression" 1894: 464). He was also listed in the school's promotional material as business manager until 1900. Whether he continued in that post beyond then is not known. From the time of her second marriage, Stebbins' name was variously cited as Genevieve Stebbins, Genevieve Stebbins Astley, or Mrs. Astley.

The prospectus for the New York School of Expression's first season (1893–1894) listed seven areas of study: literature, elocution, Delsarte expression, physiology as applied to physical culture, Swedish and aesthetic gymnastics, artistic statue posing, and dramatic criticism. It claimed to offer:

1. An artistic finishing touch for teachers and post-graduates.

2. A systematic course of instruction, for normal pupils [those seeking to be teachers], in those studies which command an immediate market value.

3. Elective courses of study, with special diplomas for graduates in Physical Culture, Delsarte Expression, or Elocution.

4. A Gymnasium specially equipped for Swedish and Aesthetic work. (*New York School of Expression* 1893)

Besides the special diplomas, students could work for a Diploma of Merit, which required successful work in the first five study areas.

Stebbins was the sole principal of the school until March 1894 when she was joined by F. Townsend Southwick, a noted reciter, teacher, and writer specializing in expression and oratory. This was actually a merger of his School of Oratory (founded ca. 1889) and the New York School of Expression. In 1901, the school was chartered by the Regents of the University of the State of New York with Southwick as president and Stebbins as vice-president. Stebbins became president and principal after Southwick's death in 1903 and remained in these positions until her retirement in 1907.[7]

Throughout the 1890s, Stebbins' professional activities gained her increasing recognition on a national level. In November 1892, she was listed on the board of directors of the newly organized National Association of Elocutionists. The following year, she was invited to serve on the Advisory Council of Physical Culture for the World's Columbian Exposition in Chicago and also to demonstrate her performance material at the event. In addition to her work at the New York School of Expression and her professional association activities, Stebbins was teaching, lecturing, and performing at colleges such as Wellesley and Ohio Wesleyan and in the cities of Boston, Philadelphia, New Haven, Cleveland, Buffalo, and Washington. She continued performing until at least 1903 (age 46); her last publication is dated 1914. A Dutch dance historian, J.W.F. Werumeus Buning, wrote in 1926 that Stebbins had "disappeared without a trace during a field trip in India" (14). In fact, Genevieve Stebbins and Norman Astley lived until at least 1933, apparently spending their last years in California.[8] I have yet to find obituaries for either.

Some reference to the Astley's activities in California comes from the membership brochure of the Church of Light, in the history of which both played a part. This church had been founded "to teach, practice and disseminate" lessons from the Brotherhood of Light, its forerunner and the source of its teachings. The brochure states that Astley, during his years in the army, had traveled broadly and lived in India where he became interested in occult studies, while Stebbins was already a member of the Brotherhood of Light when they married (The Church of Light: see also Godwin 1994: 360).

It is possible that the Astleys were actually associated with the Hermetic Brotherhood of Luxor (H. B. of L.), which the Church of Light includes in its history as a branch of the Brotherhood of Light. Joscelyn Godwin, a specialist on the occult, and his co-authors have described the H. B. of L. as an "order of practical occultism" that sought to teach people "how to lead a way of life most favorable to spiritual development" and how to work independently to develop their "occult powers" (Godwin et al. 1995: ix). Tracing its roots and sources from antiquity

(Godwin et al. 1915: 6), the H. B. of L. surfaced publicly in England ca. 1884–1886 under the leadership of Thomas Henry Burgoyne (née Thomas Henry Dalton [1855?–1895?]), who served as secretary of the Order, and two other men. It developed a strong rivalry with the Theosophical Society (established in 1875 by Helena Petrovna Blavatsky) (Godwin et al. 1995: 5, 7; Godwin 1994: xi). Its membership officially closed in 1913 (The Church of Light). It is difficult to separate the histories of the Brotherhood of Light, the Hermetic Brotherhood of Luxor, and other such groups that developed in the United States and Europe in the late nineteenth century.

The Astleys' connection with the H. B. of L. would seem probable because of their reported association with Burgoyne. The Church of Light brochure states that Stebbins and Astley enabled him to put the H. B. of L. lessons into written form by offering him the hospitality of their Carmel home and organizing financial support for the project. Originally made available only to members for a fee, the lessons were eventually published as *The Light of Egypt*. The first volume was reportedly completed while Burgoyne stayed with the Astleys and was published in 1889; the second, allegedly written posthumously by Burgoyne's spirit through the good offices of a medium, came out in 1900 (Godwin 1994: 360; Godwin et al. 1995: 38–39). There is a problem, however, with the time frame. Stebbins and Astley did not marry until 1893, so they could hardly have had a home in Carmel while Burgoyne was writing his first volume—and Stebbins was very involved with her teaching and performing in and around New York during the 1880s and 1890s. Perhaps Astley alone, or with a prior wife, was the host of Burgoyne in the 1880s. According to the Church of Light brochure, the Astleys were also acquainted with Elbert Benjamine, a founder of the Church of Light and its president until his death in 1951. He reportedly visited them and was helped by "extensive and encouraging correspondence he received from them."

In 1901, Stebbins translated into English a French translation of *An Egyptian Initiation* by Iamblichus of Chalcis (ca. 250–ca. 325). Godwin describes Iamblichus as both Neopythagorean and Neoplatonist and as one who appreciated "the ceremonies of the Mysteries, [and] set out to bring these practices under the wing of Platonism, to give them an intellectual justification, and to assimilate their gods with his own" (Godwin 1986: 25). The English translation was published in 1965 by the fervent Denver Mason, Edward Leon Bloom, from the manuscript provided him by H. O. Wagner, who had published an enlarged edition of Burgoyne's *Light of Egypt* in 1963. *An Egyptian Initiation*, was apparently an important text for the H. B. of L. and the later Church of Light.

In her writings, Stebbins demonstrated an ongoing interest in mysticism, so the connection with the H. B. of L. is not surprising. There is reference to a mysterious and unidentified friend who helped her with *Dynamic Breathing*, the most metaphysical of her works, and that might have been Burgoyne, or Astley. In Volume 2 of Burgoyne's *The Light of Egypt*, Stebbins and her *Dynamic Breathing* are cited in relation to "aspirational breathing" (1969: 175), but one must remember that this was written by Burgoyne's "medium" after his death.

Stebbins' last publication was *The Quest of the Spirit*, a manuscript by an anonymous "Pilgrim of the Way" that she edited. Its New York publisher was none other than Edgar S. Werner, who brought out so many of the Delsarte books by Stebbins and others. The author, whom she characterizes as a world traveler and Orientalist, could perhaps be Astley, but it is impossible to say. The volume presents the author's "comprehensive philosophy of life and action" with which Stebbins writes that she totally agreed (1913: 7). It contains discussions of evolution, the soul, "The Search for the Finite God," Buddha, Jesus, and other topics, and is, in fact, a "quest" for understanding of the universe, psychic and occult matters, religion, and how humans have sought to deal with the mysteries of life and death.

Many questions remain about Stebbins' life in relation to the occult and metaphysical, both before and after her retirement in 1907. Up to that year, there is a steady stream of information about her professional activities and expressions of her intellectual development in her writings. While she certainly gives indications of her spiritual quest in those writings, we know next to nothing of her personal life and activities outside the professional side. After her retirement, the mystery is even greater. It is established that she and Astley were living in Northern California, but what were they doing there? I have found no indication of their involvement in any aspects of the social or community life in the Monterey-Carmel area.

Up to the time of her retirement, Stebbins' life was typical of that of most American Delsarteans. She was a middle-class woman, well educated, apparently without financial worries, and operating as the captain of her own ship in the public sphere. Her public, of course, whether students or audience members, was overwhelmingly female. While she was twice married, her major focus was not husband and family (there is no record that she had any children), but rather her profession. In his capacity as business manager, her second husband served that profession. With the freedom from economic hardship that she enjoyed—and her intellectual and artistic knowledge and abilities—Stebbins was able to assume leadership in the development, pedagogy, and performance forms of American Delsartism. She touched countless people through her performances, teachings, and writings. Some of these, in their turn would become leaders in physical culture and dance in both the United States and Europe.[9]

NOTES

1. Biographical information of varying reliability has been gleaned from Wilbor 1887: 289–91; Shelton 1978: 35; "Delsartism in America," Parts I (Werner) and II (Thompson); Greenlee and Greenlee 2: 1099–1101; "Equipment of Our Faculty"; *New York School of Expression* 1893; Smith-Baranzini; and news items in the Werner magazines, *Action and Utterance,* and other periodicals.

2. Also noted in "Madison Square Theatre," *New York Tribune,* 24 April 1879: 5. Stebbins adopted the stage name Agnes Loring for this engagement on the advice of Mackaye's wife. Percy Mackaye, *Epoch* 1:303 n. After this production, she went back to using her own name professionally.

3. Letter from Lewis B. Monroe to Steele Mackaye, in Mackaye Archive, Dartmouth College, Box 7, Folder 5; Thompson 61.

4. Letter from Steele Mackaye to Genevieve Stebbins, dated 22 September 1879 (copy in Mackaye Archive, Dartmouth College, Box 7, Folder 5); a similar letter, dated 3 September 1879 is printed in Stebbins' *Society Gymnastics and Voice Culture* (1888), 109.

5. A letter of 17 October 1892 from Steele Mackaye to his wife complains of Stebbins' influence and characterizes her as "a very vicious young woman" who never forgave him for not continuing to engage her at the Madison Square Theatre. He claims, "[S]he has never lost an opportunity to lie about me—or to steal from me." Mackaye Archive, Dartmouth College, Box 7, Folder 5.

6. This passage is attributed to Delsarte in an 1892 book on the Delsarte system by Edward Warman (9), but I think he is probably incorrect.

7. The academic year ran from mid-October through the end of May, and summer courses at other locations were also offered. Classes were scheduled for three hours each afternoon with the mornings left free for "private work" at an additional charge. In the beginning, the school was located at Carnegie Hall with gymnastics given in a specially outfitted gymnasium on West 74th Street. In the fall of 1897, the school moved from Carnegie Hall to the Westside Branch of the Y.M.C.A. Building, 318 West 57th Street. When Stebbins retired in 1907, she turned the presidency over to a graduate of the school who had also served as vice-president for some years, Charlotte Sulley Presby (from the New York School of Expression's prospectuses, advertisements, and articles).

8. They are listed in the first and second (1926 and 1928) editions of *Polk's Salinas, Monterey and Pacific Grove Directory* as living in Monterey, and in the third and fourth (1930 and 1933) editions, now *Polk's Salinas, Monterey, Pacific Grove and Carmel City Directory,* as living in Carmel. Because there is no directory prior to 1926, and between 1933 and 1937 (in which they do not appear), it is impossible to know exactly when they came to the Monterey-Carmel area and when they left it—at death or for other reasons.

9. In *New York School of Expression* 1893: 28, Stebbins lists the following figures, among others, who had studied with her and had become well known as leaders either in Delsarte work or expression in general: Mrs. Frank Stuart Parker of Cook County Normal School; S. S. Curry; Mrs. Anna Baright Curry; Mrs. F. Fowle Adams; Mrs. Anna Randall-Diehl; Miss Minnie M. Jones; Mrs. Laura J.

Tisdale; Miss Anna Warren Story; Mrs. Emily M. Bishop, Lecturer on Delsarte at Chautauqua; and Miss Mary Adams Currier, Professor of Elocution at Wellesley (27). Numerous news items in Werner's magazines and in *Action and Utterance* attest to the professional placement of many of Stebbins' students.

Chapter 5

The Spread of American Delsartism in the United States and Europe

Although no institution bears the name of the great Frenchman, his teachings . . . have inter-penetrated all instruction, so in this country of ours, his influence extends from sea to sea. (Stebbins 1887: 259).

The kernel . . . is so truly good that it is worthwhile to introduce to German women the parts of these [Delsartean] teachings that are practically valuable. (Mensendieck 1908: 14).

THE UNITED STATES

In the last three decades of the nineteenth century, American Delsartism spread throughout the United States. Mackaye, Monroe, Alger, Stebbins, Hovey, and other leaders gave courses and lectures on the system in New York, Boston, and elsewhere. Their students taught from coast to coast in public and private educational contexts where they trained the next generation. The American Delsarteans also performed extensively and wrote prolifically. This section addresses who the Delsarteans were, what they were doing, where they were doing it, how they had been educated in the theory and practice of Delsartism, and to what extent their work contributed to its various manifestations.

There is an assortment of information available on more than 400 American teachers and performers active between 1870 and 1900 who either identified themselves as Delsarteans or acknowledged that system as a significant component of their training, their approach to performance, or their own teaching methods and materials.[1] Many had seriously studied the Delsarte system and contributed to its dissemination. Others, sometimes with only a smattering of knowledge, advertised themselves as Delsarteans to attract students or performing engagements. Another group did not claim to be adherents of the Delsarte system, but their approach and terminology demonstrate its influence in their work.

Between the 1870s and 1900, Delsarteans in the United States were teaching and performing in at least 38 states and the District of Columbia. The greatest concentration was in the Northeast, with the largest number in New York and Massachusetts (particularly in New York City and Boston). They were also numerous in Pennsylvania (particularly in Philadelphia) and in Illinois (mostly in Chicago). Los Angeles, San Francisco, and other California cities had their own Delsartean exponents, as did states from all regions of the country.

Of the teachers and performers on whom information has been collected, about 85 percent are women. Both the men and the women practiced in the field of elocution/expression except for a few in other disciplines: art history, music, sculpture, and writing. At least 20 (about 6%) of the women and 13 (about 22%) of the men were founders and/or principals of schools in which they also taught. These figures show that even in this field, men were more likely than women to assume positions of authority. Most of the others earned their living by teaching both privately and for various types of educational institutions. The American Delsarteans were typically artist/teachers rather than one or the other, so most of them performed on a regular basis, often including their students in the productions. Such events may have contributed to their incomes or been financial burdens that had to be borne to maintain professional visibility. The productions featured or included the nonverbal genres: statue poses, *tableaux mouvants*, pantomimes, and dances. They often involved elaborate costumes, sets, and props; the newly available electric lighting effects; and musical accompaniment.

Predictably, the Delsarteans, as elocutionists in general, appear to have been middle class, well educated, and highly literate. Their work required knowledge of current and past literature and elocutionary theories and trends. In addition, many had their own writings published, which contributed to their professional visibility and credibility. At least 16 (under 5%) of the women in this group and 15 (25%) of the men wrote one or more books, and for the most part, wrote them well. Again, it is interesting to note the disparity in the percentages. In addition to books, many of the Delsarteans wrote regularly for Werner's magazines and other publications. Their contributions included articles singly or in series; regular columns; letters to the editor; and creative work such as poems, recitations, and scenarios for pantomimes, drills, and other performance material.

The Delsarteans were a committed lot. In addition to expressing their opinions frequently in print, many were energetically involved in professional organizations where they shared information, debated issues of disagreement, fought to maintain standards, and promoted their field. The National Association of Elocutionists, one of the most important and influential organizations in this field, held its first meeting in 1892. A number of state associations were also formed.[2] Many of the organizations' leaders were prominent Delsarteans, but some were outspoken opponents of the system, so questions about the system were often passionately argued out at meetings.

The organizations and publications made possible much interchange and mutual influence among the Delsarteans throughout the United States. Communication was reinforced by the frequent and extensive touring that many of them did and also by the joint performances that they gave. As in the field of elocution in general, there was a common use of much of the published performance material such as recitations, pantomimes, drills, and so forth. The result of all this was that the American Delsarteans shared a large body of knowledge, theory, techniques, and performance practices.

American Delsarteans were also aware of Delsartean practitioners outside of the United States. In Werner's magazines and other publications, there was occasional information about specialists in other countries, specifically in France, England, Australia, and Canada. A few foreigners advertised in the American magazines: two Canadians; the English cleric, Joe Edgar Foster; and the last French teacher of the system who had studied with François Delsarte himself, Alfred Giraudet. A few Americans made their way to Europe. In the 1870s and early 1880s, they went to study; later some taught or performed there. A high point, of course, in the international exchange (or low point, depending on who was discussing it) was Mme. Géraldy's visit to the United States in 1892.

The most striking difference between the men and the women associated with American Delsartism is in the scope of their expressional endeavors. All were involved in performance genres in which the spoken word was primary: recitations of stories or poems, dramatic readings, play productions, and oratory. In addition, at least 25 percent of the women, but only a few of the men, also taught and presented dance or quasi-dance pieces such as statue posing, *tableaux mouvants*, pantomime, Delsartean attitudes, and drills in their recitals. Most male Delsarteans limited their presentations to mainly verbal material, using bodily expression for enhancement of a text rather than as an end in itself. While perhaps eight of the men were involved to some extent with Delsartean gymnastics, posing, drills, or *tableaux*, only one, Edward L. Barbour, predominately featured such activities in his teaching and recitals. At the Hollins Institute in Virginia, where he taught until 1891, Barbour presented his students in "aesthetic movements from Delsarte and *tableaux mouvants*" (*Werner's Voice Magazine* 13 [June 1891]: 159), and in *"poses plastiques* including Niobe group, Hebe, the Fates, Dance of the Muses, Cymbal Player, Toilet of the Bride, Bacchus and Bacchantes, Sacrifice of Iphigenia" as well as in recitations (*Werner's Voice Magazine* 13 [July 1891]: 185). Although he does not seem to have continued this kind of work at Rutgers College where he was appointed chair of Elocution and Oratory later in 1891, in 1893 Barbour presented a group of Greek-gowned high school girls in a demonstration of Delsarte and Ling movements (*Werner's Magazine* 15 [July 1893]: 258). That combination, as well as the content of his programs at the Hollins Institute, suggest that Barbour had probably studied with Stebbins.

The general outline of how the Delsarte system developed in the United States into a popular pastime for nonprofessionals in addition to its role in professional training is clear. The foundation and major line goes from François Delsarte through Steele Mackaye to a small group of Americans, most importantly, Genevieve Stebbins and Henrietta Hovey, who adapted and spread the theory and practice by means of their teaching, writing, and/or performance. In turn, their students disseminated it even further through the Delsartean heyday of the 1890s and, in some significant cases, into the twentieth century. The problem comes in trying to trace both the general education and the specific training of individual Delsarteans beyond Mackaye, Stebbins, and Hovey. There is information about some of the leading figures, however, and a look at a few of them will add human faces to the statistical data and further illuminate the spread of the Delsarte system in the United States.

Emily M. Bishop (1858–1916)

Emily (or Mrs. Coleman E.) Bishop influenced the development of American Delsartism on the national level through her teaching, publications, and other professional activities. In her 1892 *Americanized Delsarte Culture* Bishop wrote that she began her study of the Delsarte system in 1881 under "an enthusiastic artist-teacher, Frances Chamberlain Streeter" (1892a, Appendix i–ii). She must have been a student of Mackaye, Monroe, or Alger to have been teaching at such an early date. Stebbins claimed that Bishop had been her student (*New York School of Expression* 1893: 27), but Bishop makes no mention of this. Whatever the nature of her training, Bishop became an important leader in the development and dissemination of American Delsartism. She was active from the 1880s to at least 1901.

While Bishop taught at times in Brooklyn, Canada, and perhaps other locations, her main venue was Chautauqua in southwestern New York State, the site of an important development in nineteenth-century American adult education.[3] The original Chautauqua summer session was offered in 1874 as a Sunday School teacher's assembly. From that beginning evolved what one historian has described as "a bewildering variety of activities in education, religion, discussion of public issues, music, art, theater, sports, hobbies, and clubs" (Morrison 1974: vii). In time the term "Chautauqua" came to designate not only the institute on Lake Chautauqua in New York, but also "imitative assemblies" that were established throughout the United States and "traveling tent companies" that toured various kinds of programs around the country (Morrison 1974: vii). It was the summer institute at the New York Chautauqua site where Bishop taught. At this location, what began in 1874 as a 15-day program had grown by 1899 to 60 days and was attracting thousands of participants from across the United States and even from abroad (Morrison 1974: 42–47). A department of physical culture was established in 1886 under the direction of Dr. William G. Anderson, a noted physical education specialist, who assembled a faculty of other distinguished educators from various institutions. Bishop was engaged in 1888 to teach the Delsartean gymnastic exercises without the more expressive aspects of the system (Wilbor 1890). By 1891, oppositions, successions, and statue posing (see Part II) were also being taught to the advanced class, and in 1894, a full-fledged Chautauqua School of Expression was established with Bishop as co-principal with the elocutionist S. J. Clark of the University of Chicago.

In its early years the Delsarte work at Chautauqua served mainly as a general educational experience for nonprofessionals. Thus one reporter described the 1891 Chautauqua students as "composed largely of mature women, not in public life, but mothers, grandmothers, and teachers of experience and prominence. We find among them a few gentlemen, physicians and ministers; and a number of society girls who are sensible and brave enough to appreciate health and grace" (Morris 1891: 253). In contrast, an 1894 advertisement includes the following statistics (from the *Chautauqua Assembly Herald* of 24 August 1894): of a total enrollment of 257, 27 were elocution teachers in institutions of higher education; 58 were public school teachers; 20 were private school teachers; 14 were ministers; and the rest were unclassified (*Werner's Magazine* 16 [December]). This suggests that the training was serving more and more as professional preparation, but in this context it appealed to professional educators rather than actors or orators. Of the total number of students that year, approximately 30 percent were involved in public or private schools and 10 percent in universities. Thus the system would spread throughout the nation.

Bishop's 1892 *Americanized Delsarte Culture*, which came out in several editions, provided instruction in Delsartean physical culture for the promotion of health and grace in everyday life. After briefly discussing Delsarte's life and work and what distinguished Americanized Delsarte work from other physical culture approaches, Bishop gave guidance and exercises for improving bodily activities such as standing, sitting, rising, breathing, and relaxation. She also discussed common health problems such as obesity, insomnia, nervousness, and illness and how to avoid the debilities of old age. This book was clearly written for the nonprofessional, but Bishop's interest was not limited to that. In her teaching of professionals as well as nonprofessionals at Chautauqua, her active involvement with the National Association of Elocutionists (including giving presentations at conferences), and her writings for *Werner's Magazine*, she contributed to the development and dissemination of Delsartism for the performer and teacher as well as for the layperson.

R. Anna Morris

One of those who studied with Bishop at Chautauqua in the summer of 1891 was R. Anna Morris. She supervised the physical culture and declamation programs for the Des Moines, Iowa, public school system from at least the late 1880s, and then physical culture for primary grades and teacher training for the Cleveland public schools from 1894 until at least 1900. In 1891, Morris was not a novice Delsartean. She had published a book in 1888, *Physical Culture in the Public Schools*, that was based on Delsarte principles "as taught by Mrs. A. C. Gunter, *née* Etta L. Burns, Mrs. Henrietta Crane Russel [*sic*] and Genevieve Stebbins," and on exercises developed by Dr. W. G. Anderson. In addition to her work in grade school and teacher training, Morris was active in a number of ways. She performed recitations; spoke publicly for dress reform in Iowa and other locations; organized teacher institutes; presented students (both boys and girls) in performances of drills, mythological plays, *tableaux*, statue posing, pantomimes, and Delsartean attitudes; and in 1898, she taught physical culture and Delsarte expression at the Ohio Chautauqua.

Morris' book was written as a guide for teachers and students. It begins with instructions for sitting positions, rising, standing positions, breathing, and arm movements before introducing well-known American Delsartean exercises for decomposing, harmonic poise, walking, and "feather movements." The next section develops the Delsartean material into exercises for different grades. Subsequent chapters give work on marching, exercises with wands and clubs, fencing movements with sticks, Delsartean "attitudes," and declamation. In this book, as in her statements elsewhere, Morris demonstrated her eclectic approach to physical training. Delsarte was a major element, but she also used material from other sources as well, including the German Jahn and Swedish Ling gymnastics systems.

While Morris' major work and sphere of influence was on the local level, she also gained national visibility through her occasional writing for Werner's magazines, her presentations for organizations such as the California State Teachers Association, and her involvement with the National Educational Association. It was teachers such as Morris who promoted movement as a healthy and respectable activity to countless numbers of children and adults throughout the country.

Eva Allen Alberti

Eva Allen Alberti, described in *Werner's Voice Magazine* as "one of the best Delsarteans in the profession,"[4] was teaching in New York City and at summer locations in New Jersey from at least the mid- or late 1880s. She and her husband, William M. Alberti, headed what they called "Madame Alberti's Delsarte School of Expression," an educational institution for female boarding or day students, which moved into spacious new quarters on Fifth Avenue about January 1892. According to the school's prospectus, covering 1893–1894 and 1894–1895, the courses offered a broad range of study: Aesthetic Gymnastics; Universal Literature in Enlish; Expression; Physiological Psychology; Anatomy; Physiology; Hygiene; Games; Statue Poses; Science of Beauty; Art, History, Foreign Travel; and Special and Elective Studies, including art, music, languages, dancing, fencing, and "any needed subject." Aesthetic Gymnastics included not only physical culture from Delsarte, Ling, and what she termed "eclectic" sources, but also two components called Society Culture and Society Forms. Perhaps these latter were social dances and ballroom etiquette. Under the rubric of Expression she offered elocution based on Delsarte, White, and again "eclectic" materials. Madame Alberti taught the Delsarte system, elocution, and physical culture, while her husband taught Delsartean Theory and Physiological Psychology. Other faculty members taught the remaining subjects.

In the realm of performance Alberti herself was best known for her recitations, and especially for her songs pantomimed in "deaf-mute language." She was particularly praised for her renditions of the hymn "Nearer, My God to Thee" and the "Star Spangled Banner." Alberti regularly presented her students in plays, pantomimes, and dances, as well as recitations. On 29 May 1891, for example, she directed them in Sophocles *Electra* for Brooklyn's Friday Afternoon Reading Club. The short review notes that the performers "went through the various dances and the pantomime work unusually well for amateurs." It praises the original music composed for the event and adds that "various colored lights, corresponding with the emotions being depicted, were thrown on the stage" (*Werner's Voice Magazine* 13 [July 1891]: 186). Another such item, presented 18 December 1891, was a "Hellenic dance" performed by eight young women in Greek costumes, who manipulated gauze scarves as they danced (*Werner's Voice Magazine* 14 [January 1892]: 30).

In the school brochure, Alberti stated that she had acquired her training from "the great teachers Delsarte, White [?], Monroe, and their followers." It would, of course, not have been possible for her to have studied with François Delsarte, and it is hardly likely that she had studied with Gustave, so probably she received her training from those who had themselves trained with the father or son, perhaps Mackaye, Alger, or Hovey. Alberti also attributes her knowledge and qualifications to study of "the noble works of Darwin, Spencer, Mantegazza, Froebel, Clifford, Sir C. Bell, Austin, Guttman, Rush, Russell, Bell, Browne and Behnke" (Alberti 1894: 11), assuming that the reader would be familiar with these names and be impressed. It will be remembered that Darwin and Mantegazza were featured along with Delsarte in Moses True Brown's book on the Delsarte system.

There is evidence that Alberti taught many who would carry on the work. Two teachers who made particular use of her Delsartean "movements, poses, attitudes" and her Greek dance were Jessie Ellis, head of the departments of elocution and physical culture at the Young Ladies Seminary in Hollidaysburg, Pennsylvania, and Mrs. Oscar Denton, a Mississippian who taught and performed all over the South. An important twentieth-century pioneer in dance education who learned from Alberti was Gertrude Colby, who developed "natural dance" for the progressive education curriculum at Teachers College, Columbia University, where she taught from 1913 to 1931 (O'Donnell 1936: 1, 8; Ruyter 1979: 111–15). In 1913, "The Conflict; A Health Masque in Pantomime," which was presented by Colby at Teachers College, included pantomime set by Alberti (Colby 1930: 7–8).

Alberti was enthusiastically praised in many references in Werner's magazines and seemed to enjoy universal esteem. In 1892, she was elected corresponding secretary of the New York Teachers of Oratory, and in 1894 served on the board of examiners for Stebbins' New York School of Expression. She also belonged to the National Association of Elocutionists.

Eleanor Georgen

A native of Philadelphia, Eleanor (or Ella) Georgen received her first elocutionary training there in 1880.[5] She was apparently a gifted platform reader as she spent two seasons touring Canada and New York after her initial study. Georgen then moved to New York City and embarked on an acting career. Enrollment in the Lyceum School of Acting, which had been founded in 1884 by Steele Mackaye and Franklin H. Sargent, brought her into contact with the Delsarte system. She studied it under

Ida Serven and Sargent. After a few roles on the professional stage, Georgen decided to give up acting and devote herself to teaching. In 1887 she was appointed head of elocution, pantomime, and the Delsarte system at the New York School of Acting, the former Lyceum School, now headed by Sargent without Mackaye's participation. Georgen remained on the staff of this institution (renamed the American Academy of Dramatic Arts in 1892) until 1897 or 1898, when she left to found another institution with a prominent actor/educator named F. F. Mackay and apparently her own independent school as well. The resulting National Dramatic Conservatory and the Georgen Aesthetic and Dramatic School were advertised at the same address in New York City. Until her retirement in 1899, Georgen was also active in the field of elocution as a reader and author. She was a founding member of the National Association of Elocutionists.

In 1893, Georgen's book, *The Delsarte System of Physical Culture,* was published. In her introduction, Georgen writes that the Delsarte system's gymnastics were "designed to strengthen and relax every muscle of the body" and consitute "the most nearly perfect form of physical culture that we have." She notes that while some gymnastics training is "too violent for girls and women," the Delsarte exercise program is good for all in its promotion of health and youth (Introduction). The book, with an endorsement by Sargent, is clearly based on Mackaye's teachings. It includes discussions about and exercises for poise, relaxation, flexibility, strength, walking, transitions, deportment, expressive formulas, and gestures. Like much of the American Delsartean literature, it was designed more for the general population than for professional training. It received praise from no less an authority than F. Townsend Southwick (Stebbins' partner in the New York School of Expression), who was usually more prone to criticize than appreciate his colleagues. Even though he considered it incomplete because Georgen did not include the philosophical principles underlying the practical work, he still concluded that her book was one of the best ("Topics of the Month" 15 [November 1893]: 381). Georgen also served on the examining board for the New York School of Expression in 1894.

Mary Perry King (1865–ca. 1930)

Born in Oswego, New York, Mary Perry married Morris Lee King in 1887.[6] She was a graduate of Oswego Normal College and the Philadelphia College of Oratory and reportedly also trained in physical expression and vocal culture in Paris and London. Ted Shawn states that King had studied the Delsarte system with Henrietta Hovey (1974: 12). Hovey had taught at Oswego, probably in the 1880s, and it is clear that King's orientation was Delsartean, although she never claimed this designation and did not acknowledge specific teachers. King taught in New York and elsewhere and established in New Canaan, Connecticut, the School of Personal Harmonizing, which has been variously designated "Uni-Trinian" (Terry 1969: 97), "Triunian" (Shelton 1981: 119; Kendall 1979: 110), and "Uni-trinitarian" (*Who's Who in America* 1912–1913: 1176). She enjoyed a close collaboration with the poet Bliss Carman, and he acknowledged her as his collaborator in *The Making of Personality* (1908: viii), which is based on Delsartean principles. Carman was close friends with Richard Hovey, and with Henrietta after their marriage, and reportedly had learned about the Delsarte system from her. Besides teaching, King wrote a number of books and articles and presented lectures on topics such as personal charm, poetic dancing, the natural woman, and women of the Orient (the latter in an "oriental" costume). She is best known in the context of dance history because of Ted Shawn. He had read an article by Carman, also titled "The Making of a Personality." It reflected so completely Shawn's own feelings and thoughts that he wrote to Carman asking where he could study dance based on such ideas. Carman recommended King (Shawn 1974: 11–12), and this became Shawn's introduction to Delsartean theory and practice (although, again, it was not identified as such).

Both King and Carman focused on how to make life better, not necessarily how to train artists, but their writings, as so much of the Delsartean *oeuvre*, could be used as either life training or art training, and to most of the Delsarteans, there did not seem to be much difference between the two. King's *Comfort and Exercise* of 1900 is subtitled *An Essay toward Normal Conduct* and includes chapters on comfort in general, in daily life, in education, and in dress; and on educational exercise and the ideal gymnasium. She begins on the lofty plain of "the informing spirit of beauty and truth" and "some fresh stir towards goodness and the liberation of the soul" (3) and soon arrives at the threefold nature of the human being: the spirit, mind, and body (6). Comfort rests on what she terms "equal respect" for the three aspects (12–13).

Delsartean teachers such as these were important in spreading the theory and practice to a broad public of mainly women and children. Their books served as treatises for teaching or practice. Their contributions, however, were not as far reaching as those of Stebbins, because they basically stayed within the limits of the already known while Stebbins pushed at those limits and developed new directions.

EUROPE

The American adaptation of Delsarte's theory and practice was not only a factor in women's lives and physical expression in the United States; but it also traveled or was carried back to Europe in the early twentieth century where it fed into already emerging new directions in physical culture and dance. It is unclear how American Delsartism first came to the attention of European physical culturists. Perhaps it was by means of its specialized and numerous publications. As early as 1899, an advertisement for Emily M. Bishop's 1892 *Americanized Delsarte Culture* includes a testimonial from a Harriet Davis Güssbacher of Berlin. She states that she is introducing the Delsarte system into Germany where the "people have never heard of aesthetic gymnastics nor of influencing the mind at the same time with the body" (*Werner's Magazine* 23, nos. 3–8 [1899]: back of bound volume). Presumably, Bishop's text would serve as her source. Evidence that the Delsarte system was known in Finland through the works of Stebbins is provided by Saga Ambegaokar in her thesis on the Finnish modern dance pioneer Maggie Gripenberg (Ambegaokar 133). Moreover in 1913, a Russian treatise on the Delsarte system by Prince Sergei Mikhailovich Volkonsky was published and listed 23 Delsarte texts in French, German, and English, including Stebbins' four books and 12 other works by American Delsarteans. Clearly, American Delsartean literature was known in Europe.[7] Volkonsky's two German references are the Mensendieck and Kallmeyer texts discussed below, which shows that knowledge at least of Stebbins' work was spreading not only through her own publications, but also through the writings of Europeans. Mensendieck and Kallmeyer are key figures in the Central European connection with Stebbins and the Delsarte system. Through their work and that of their students, it spread widely in physical culture and dance contexts.

Bess Mensendieck (1864–1958)

Although born and initially educated in New York, Dr. Bess Mensendieck spent much of her life in Europe where she completed her medical degree at the University of Zurich and worked to develop physical training for both medical and general educational purposes. She studied specific approaches with various specialists in France and Germany as well as with Genevieve Stebbins in the United States and developed a program of "functional exercises." She based her system on the scientific study of anatomy and physiology and what she considered to be the natural laws under which they operate. Her goal was to instill a conscious awareness of muscular function, and to this end, she developed exercises to counteract faulty use. She distinguished between dance and gymnastics and focused her attention on the latter. Her work became widely known through the Mensendieck training centers she established in Germany, Austria, the Netherlands, Denmark, Czechoslovakia, and New York and through books and essays that she published in both German and English (Brown and Sommer 39–41, 52; Toepfer 41).

Mensendieck's first contact with the Delsarte system may have been during her youth in New York, since by her teen years, American Delsartism was gaining more and more visibility and adherents. It might also have been through an early German proponent such as Güssbacher or from American publications that she first learned something about the system. In any case, she reportedly studied with Stebbins (Lämmel 39; Toepfer 40), probably in 1906 or earlier.[8]

Mensendieck's *Körperkultur des Weibes* (Women's Physical Culture) was written about the time she worked with Stebbins and shows that influence more clearly than later writings. Originally published in 1906 with revised editions in 1907 and 1908, this work provides ample evidence of Mensendieck's familiarity with the American Delsarte system, her admiration of it, and her appropriation of some of its aspects. In a section on the care of the body in America, she writes that as early as the 1870s, American women were beginning to study physical culture in relation to the female body and attributes that interest to the introduction and development of the Delsarte system in the United States (1908: 11). She declares that American women have particularly graceful demeanor due to the Delsarte work and that "the American woman gains recognition everywhere" for this quality (1908: 13).

Mensendieck criticizes both Delsarte and Stebbins for emphasizing beauty, or the aesthetic, without giving primary attention to health, the subject that most interested her (1908: 13); but she also commends Stebbins for combining the Delsartean theory and practice with the Swedish Ling gymnastics to create "astonishing results in the perfection of the body in terms of health and aesthetics" and for developing a practical methodology for "domestic use" (1908: 12). She highly praises the success of the method on Stebbins herself, writing, "After years of earnest efforts she could demonstrate on her own body through these special exercises how many different beautiful forms a woman could attain through working by herself, that grace is not a natural gift, but rather a miracle which is in the power of every woman to evoke" (1908: 12). It should be noted that Stebbins would have been close to 50 years old when Mensendieck studied with her and was probably an unusually fit woman for that age in either the United States or Europe.

Mensendieck also complained that elements she considered metaphysical and thus "blooming nonsense" had crept into the American Delsarte work through Mackaye and Stebbins and through "the odd inclination of the American mind to enlarge upon aesthetics . . . toward the metaphysical side" (1908: 14). This is not quite accurate as the metaphysical aspect was there from the beginning, in Delsarte's own work. She might, however, be referring to the Delsarteans' propensity to contextualize the specific in universal terms and to Stebbins' enthusiasm for yoga and other non-Western disciplines that she combined with the Delsarte and Ling material. Despite her criticisms, however, Mensendieck's overall assessment of what she learned from Stebbins is very positive. Because she considered it so valuable, she included what she called "this American preparatory work" in *Körperkultur des Weibes* (14), which reportedly was influential in women's physical education in Germany as late as the 1930s (Toepfer 39).

Delsarte/Mackaye/Stebbins elements can be found throughout Mensendieck's first book, but as one would expect, she emphasized practical physical training for health and strength rather than for use in expressive endeavors. In her list of the necessary components for training, Mensendieck included: (1) the saving of strength (economy of movement); (2) mastery of the total scope of movement; (3) space awareness; (4) the execution of lines; (5) rhythm; (6) weight; (7) breathing; (8) energizing; and (9) relaxation (1908: 28). While all of these are at least implicit in Stebbins' training methodology, even if conceptualized in somewhat different terms, the last three are particularly central.

Mensendieck discussed each of the nine elements in detail and used reproductions of art works depicting human figures (as did Stebbins) to illustrate principles of body position. In a few cases, Mensendieck even chose the same statues included in the 1902 sixth edition of Stebbins' *Delsarte System of Expression*, but to different purpose. While Stebbins presented them as models for statue posing, Mensendieck had a point to make with each.

Hade Kallmeyer (1881–?)

In contrast to Mensendieck, who combined her learning from many sources with independent research to create a new system under her own name, Hade Kallmeyer identified her work so closely with Stebbins that she termed it the "American Stebbins-Kallmeyer System" in her published writings.[9] Kallmeyer also differs from Mensendieck in that she enjoyed less international and continuing visibility. While Mensendieck is referred to in many works in both English and German on the history of physical education and her publications can be found in American libraries as well as in those of Europe, Kallmeyer is less frequently mentioned and her two books are virtually unobtainable in the United States. Hade Kallmeyer (sometimes referred to as Heda Kallmeyer, Hedwig Kallmeyer, or Hedwig Kallmeyer-Simon) was born in the early 1880s in Stuttgart. What is known about her training (from her own testimony) is that she studied English calisthenics in London in 1905 and the Delsarte system with Genevieve Stebbins in New York in 1906 (Kallmeyer 1910: 2–4; Brown and Sommer 52; Toepfer 147). After returning to Germany, she opened a school of "harmonic gymnastics" in Berlin where she reportedly "introduced the Stebbins method into Germany" (Brown and Sommer 52, citing Kallmeyer statement of 1926).

Kallmeyer published two works on the "Stebbins-Kallmeyer System," *Künstlerische Gymnastik* (Artistic Gymnastics) in 1910, and *Schönheit und Gesundheit des Weibes durch Gymnastik* (Beauty and Health for Women through Gymnastics) in 1911. The two books are nearly identical. After the introductory material that surveys the field of physical culture and introduces Genevieve Stebbins and her work, *Künstlerische Gymnastik* includes sections on "harmonic education," posture; the three fundamentals of breathing, relaxation, and muscle stretching; and Delsarte's three laws of motion: harmonic poise, opposition, and succession. Some 40 pages of exercises from *The Genevieve Stebbins System of Physical Training* follows, including drills such as "oriental prayer" (Stebbins' "Eastern Temple Drill"); a May dance (derived from the "English Drill"); and a combining of statue poses of Amazon, Nymph, and Victory that resembles Stebbins' "Athenian Drill."

A survey of physical culture published in 1926 states that Kallmeyer was "the most prominent student of Genevieve Stebbins" and repeats the claim that in 1908, after returning home from the United States, she was the first one in Germany to present the idea of physical education on an artistic basis (Preiss 22). A 1928 work on modern dance states that her influence was significant because she taught several who became important teachers in the development of dance and rhythmic activities in Germany (Lämmel 45).

What I like to think of as the genealogy of the American Delsartean contribution to German physical culture and dance is complicated by the fact that all sorts of influences were co-mingling at the same time: Delsarte, Dalcroze, Bode, Laban, the Elizabeth Duncan School, and others. It is not possible to separate the strands, but one can establish that through the work of Kallmeyer and Mensendieck, the American Delsartean principles and practices were at least known by the players and followed by many. Several of their students became important leaders in German movement education. For example, Elsa Gindler (1895–1961), who had studied with Kallmeyer, trained many students, at least one of whom, Sophie Ludwig, was still teaching in Berlin in the 1960s (Brown and Sommer 52–53). The famous Loheland School for Gymnastics, Agriculture and Handicraft was established after World War I by Hedwig von Rohden, a graduate of the Kallmeyer school, and Louise Langgaard, a graduate of the Mensendieck school. Loheland existed at least into the 1960s, and its graduates taught internationally (Brown and Sommer 53; Toepfer 117). The separate department of body training, established in 1921 in the Dalcroze School, was directed by Czech choreographer Jarmilla Kröschlova, a graduate of both the Dalcroze and Mensendieck schools (Brown and Sommer 55; Toepfer 41, 120). Finally, in 1925, the German Gymnastic Bund was formed. Original members included the schools of Kallmeyer, Mensendieck, Gindler, and Loheland, all of which had absorbed some degree of Stebbins' teaching (Brown and Sommer 56–57).

The aspects of American Delsartism introduced into Germany by Mensendieck and Kallmeyer were primarily those "gymnastics" developed by the American Delsarteans on the foundation of Delsarte's theory. The emphasis was thus on the facility and quality of movement rather than on the Delsartean canon of expressive gestures or attitudes. Relaxation, breathing, flow, controlled energy use, postural balance, and graceful comportment of the body thus were the goals, not a rigid vocabulary of expression. These physical culture, as opposed to expressive, elements were just as relevant to the exploration of women's bodily experiences and control in Europe as in the United States, but also they were just as easily brought into the study and development of dance as a performance art.

NOTES

1. Data for this chapter, unless otherwise noted, was gleaned primarily from news items, advertisements, and articles in Werner's magazines and other periodicals. There were probably many more proponents of Delsartism than can be determined by the spotty information that is available.

2. For information on the associations, see Werner 1896; and articles and announcements regularly in the Werner magazines from 1892 on.

3. Information on Chautauqua from Morrison 1974; Wilbor 1890; Daymon 1891; Ray 1962; Morris 1891.

4. *Werner's Voice Magazine* 13 (April 1891): 109. Information on Alberti is gleaned from small news items in Werner's magazines and from Alberti 1894.

5. Biographical information from "Eleanor Georgen" and news items from Werner's magazines, 1887–1899.

6. Bits of information on King can be found in *Who's Who in America* from 1901–1902 until several years after her death ca. 1930; Shawn 1974; Shelton 1981; Kendall 1979.

7. At least one Russian exponent of Delsartism is known: Ellen Tels (Ellen Rabanek, 1885–1994). See Toepfer 179–82; and Tels 1935.

8. Sources for Mensendieck's connection with Delsartism and/or Stebbins: Brandenburg 10; Levinson 147; Buning 14; Fischer 213–15; Giese 112–14, 116–17, 135; Giese und Hagemann; Lämmel 39–45, 47; Preiss 23; Toepfer 40, 147–48.

9. Sources for Kallmeyer's connection with Delsartism and/or Stebbins: Böhme 9; Buning 14, 33; Giese 112–13; Kallmeyer's two books; Lämmel 45; Preiss 22; Toepfer 147–48.

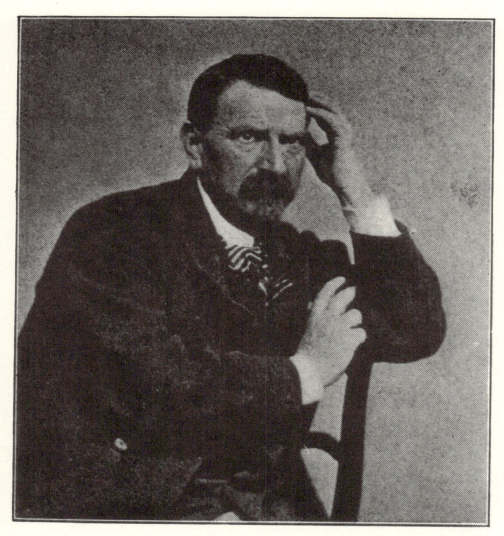

Illustration 1. François Delsarte, ca. 1869 (P. Mackaye 1927 I: facing 152).

Illustration 2. Steele Mackaye (P. Mackaye 1927 I: facing 130).

Illustration 3. Henrietta Hovey (reproduced from the Richard Hovey Collection by courtesy of the Dartmouth College Library).

Illustration 4. Genevieve Stebbins, 1892 (New York School of Expression 1893 prospectus. Courtesy of the Library of Congress).

EXCENTRIC Excentric	NORMAL Excentric	CONCENTRIC Excentric
EXCENTRIC Normal	NORMAL Normal	CONCENTRIC Normal
EXCENTRIC Concentric	NORMAL Concentric	CONCENTRIC Concentric

Illustration 5. The Ninefold Accord (Shawn 1974: 30). Delaumosne (1893: 5) and Stebbins (1902: 115) gave the same chart, but in different arrangements.

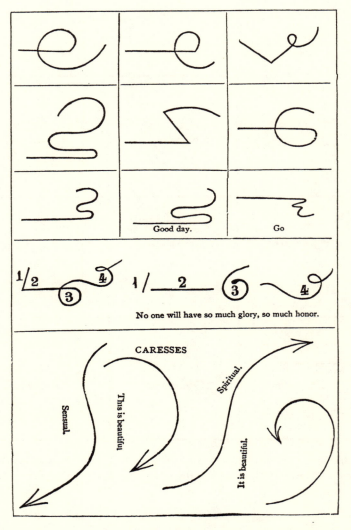

Within the illustration the following labels appear:

Good day.

Go

No one will have so much glory, so much honor.

CARESSES

Sensual.

This is beautiful.

Spiritual.

It is beautiful.

Illustration 6. Gesture: Criterion of Chorography (Delau-mosne 1893: 118).

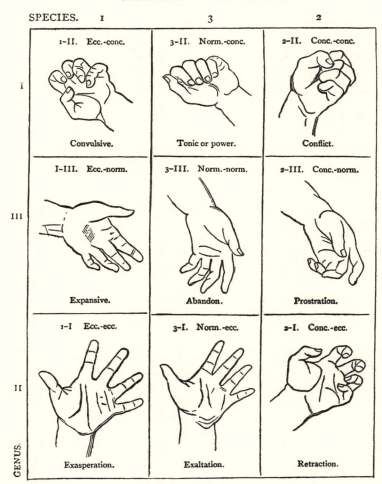

Illustration 7. Criterion of the Hand (Delaumosne 1893: 94). Stebbins (1902: 181) used Delaumosne's drawings, but arranged them according to her version of the Ninefold Accord (similar to Giraudet 1895: plate XIX).

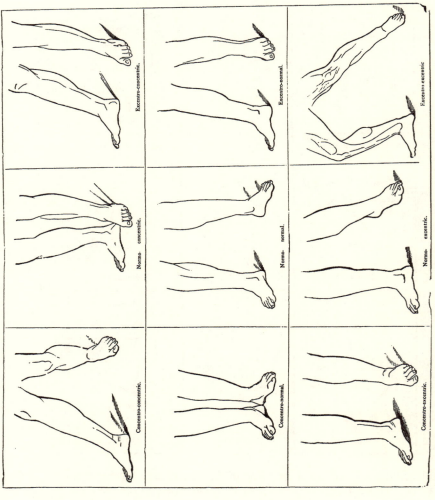

Illustration 8. Attitudes of the legs and feet while standing (Stebbins 1902: 152–53). This chart is adapted from Delaumosne (1893: following 106). Some of the attitudes are the same, while others differ.

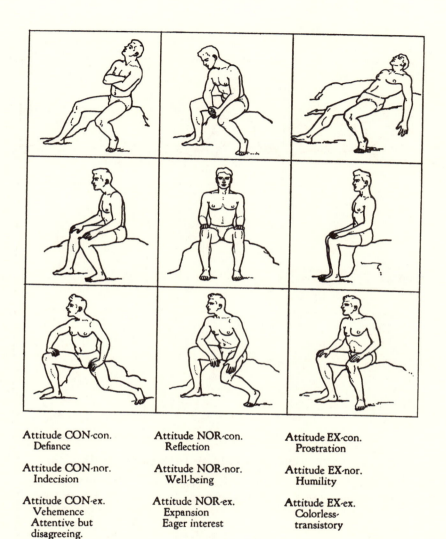

Attitude CON-con. Defiance	Attitude NOR-con. Reflection	Attitude EX-con. Prostration
Attitude CON-nor. Indecision	Attitude NOR-nor. Well-being	Attitude EX-nor. Humility
Attitude CON-ex. Vehemence Attentive but disagreeing.	Attitude NOR-ex. Expansion Eager interest	Attitude EX-ex. Colorless- transitory

Illustration 9. Attitudes of the leg while seated (Shawn 1974: 114, from Gi-raudet 1895: plate XXV). Note the inconsistency with other charts.

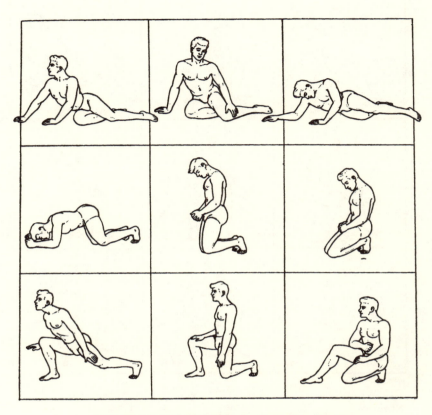

ATTITUDES OF THE LEGS—kneeling and on the side.

Att. CON-ex.	Att. CON-nor.	Att. CON-con
Vanquished but with hope of return	Weakness	Vanquished with no hope of return
Att. NOR-ex.	Att. NOR-nor	Att. NOR-con
Submission Obeisance	Humility	Discouragement
Att. EX-ex.	Att. EX-nor	Att. EX-con
Offensive Attack	Passive Colorless	Defensive

Illustration 10. Attitudes of legs while kneeling and on the floor (Shawn 1974: 113, from Giraudet 1895: plate XXIV). Again, note the inconsistency.

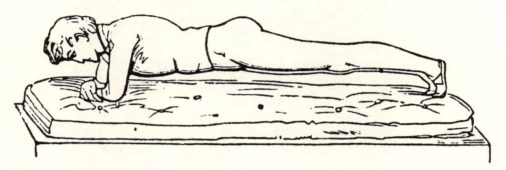

Exercise 61. Elbows-and-toes lying, holding

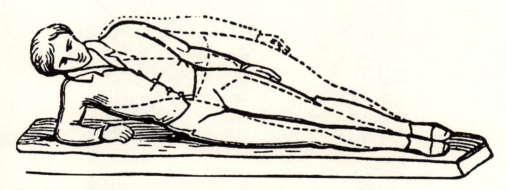

Exercise 62. Elbow-and-leg sidewise-lying, hips raising

Illustration 11. Two Swedish gymnastic exercises Stebbins learned from her studies with George H. Taylor (1860, 1879a, 220, 221).

Illustration 12. Mercury Belvedere from the Vatican (reproduced in Stebbins 1902: 324). This statue illustrates the Delsartean "harmonic poise" that figured so prominently in Stebbins' work.

Illustration 13. Diana Shooting a Bow from the National Museum, Naples (reproduced in Stebbins 1902: 169). This work served as an action model for statue posing.

Illustration 14. Discobolus (Quoit Thrower) from the Vatican (reproduced in Stebbins 1902: 170). A male in action, used as a model for statue posing.

Illustration 15. Group with a Gaul from Villa Ludovisi, Rome (reproduced in Stebbins 1902: 272). An example of the violence depicted in some of the models used for statue posing.

Illustration 16. Atalanta from the Louvre (reproduced in Stebbins 1902: 80). Another action pose.

Illustration 17. Crouching Venus from the Vatican (reproduced in Stebbins 1902: 131). One assumes a statue poser's
thighs must have had some strength to get into and out of
this kind of pose.

PART II

AMERICAN DELSARTEAN THEORY AND PRACTICE

Chapter 6

The Delsarte-Mackaye System

Gesture corresponds to the soul, to the heart; language to the life, to the thought, to the mind. The life and the mind being subordinate to the heart, to the soul, gesture is the chief organic agent. (François Delsarte, in *Delsarte System of Oratory* 1893: 465).

The aim of this system is to bestow upon the student an intelligent and aesthetic possession of all his physical resources of expression; to place completely under his command that marvelous instrument of emotion, the human body; to gradually develop an instinctive, spontaneous, and unconscious conformity to principles of harmony and perfection in physical motion. (Steele Mackaye 1875: 12–13)

DELSARTE

Since Delsarte never wrote a treatise on his system, our knowledge of it must rely on his fragmentary "literary remains" and the publications and notes of those who had studied with him. Delsarte's written materials include the prospectus for a book that would trace the development of his ideas (in Porte 1992: 55–88; and *Delsarte System of Oratory* 384–447); his 1865 address before the Philotechnic Society (in Stebbins 1902: 21–68; excerpt in Porte 192–201); and fragmentary notes and diagrams published in Porte and in *Delsarte System of Oratory*. Writings of his students include not only the books of Delaumosne, Arnaud, and Giraudet, but also some of the detailed notebooks made by those who attended his *Cours d'esthetique appliquée*. A few of these are in the Delsarte Archive at Louisiana State University, and one has been translated into English (Levy 1940). In addition, there is a wealth of manuscript material written by Mackaye. Secondary material includes publications by both practitioners and critics of American Delsartism in the late nineteenth century, and twentieth-century writings of which the most important is that of Ted Shawn (1974). While all accounts differ somewhat in emphasis, in what is included and omitted, and in details, they all agree on the general theory, aesthetics, and outline of Delsarte's system.

Delsarte's investigation into expression had grown out of his frustration with the lack of organization and consistency in his Paris Conservatory training, and it reflected both practical and theoretical concerns. On the one hand, he wanted to base his work on the realities of "nature." To this end he studied how people in everyday situations express character and emotion and how the instruments of expression (body, voice, and breath) actually function. He conducted research, observing people in all kinds of situations, even in death or during the process of dying. On the other hand, Delsarte sought basic principles underlying what was specific and individual, universals that he was sure existed.

The practical side of Delsarte's research resulted in a myriad of details about the expression of both character and emotion in each minute part of the face and body as well as an approach to training the "agents" of expression: the voice, gesture, and speech. The theoretical side led to a number of "laws" or principles upon which the training was based, and it is this aspect of his work that is most interesting today, with some of it still relevant in the contexts of dancer and actor training. Fundamental to Delsarte's system were his Law of Correspondence and Law of Trinity. Both of these suggest influence from Emanuel Swedenborg (1899–1772) whose doctrine postulated correspondence between two aspects of life—the visible outer world and the invisible spiritual realm—and three spheres—the natural, spiritual, and divine.

Delsarte's Law of Correspondence concerns the relationship between tangible and intangible, outer and inner, movement and meaning. Rejecting the idea of a division between lofty mind and lowly body, it rehabilitates the concept of the body into a worthy whole that includes the mental, emotional, and spiritual aspects of existence. Commitment to the idea of correspondence between the physical and nonphysical realms was a common theme, not only in Delsartean literature, but also in that of various writers on physical culture, nontraditional medicine, expression, and other subjects in the nineteenth century.

In Delsarte's 1865 address before the Philotechnic Society, he expressed his Law of Correspondence thus: "To each spiritual function responds a function of the body. To each grand function of the body, corresponds a spiritual act" (in Stebbins 1902: 67). What this means in practical terms is that any thought, intention, psychological state, character trait, or emotion—"spiritual function"—will have bodily manifestations; and conversely, that gesture, facial expression, voice, carriage, physical mannerism, bodily rhythm, and breathing—or any "function of the body"—cannot help but reflect, express, and even engender aspects of the "spiritual function." In other words position or movement of the body as a whole, or its parts, is in an integral, two-way connection with states of mind, feelings, and intentions. This idea would be fundamental to twentieth-century actor training methodology as developed and practiced by major figures such as Constantin Stanislavsky in his "method of physical actions" (see Moore 1967: 73–75; Moore 1968: 6–7); Jerzy Grotowski (see Grotowski 1969: 133–72); and Eugenio Barba (see Christoffersen 1993: 78–80).

Delsarte's other fundamental principle, the Law of Trinity, is the most problematic element in his theory. The Christian Trinity provided the model for what Delsarte believed was "a universal formula which may be applied to all sciences, to all things possible." To form a trinity, he explained, "three expressions are requisite, each presupposing and implying the other two. . . . There must also be an absolute co-necessity between them. Thus the three principles of our being life, mind and soul form a trinity" (quoted in Stebbins 1902: 111). In another passage, he defined a trinity as "the unity of three things, each of which is essential to the other two, each co-existing in time, co-penetrating in space, and co-operative in motion" (quoted in Shawn 1974: 28).

In Delsarte's view the number of trinities in the universe was infinite and each element of every trinity belonged to one of three categories. It was "excentric," moving out from the center; "normal," the center itself; or "concentric," moving toward the center. Here are some examples of his trinities and their designations:

excentric	normal	concentric
life	soul	mind
physical	moral	mental
vital	spiritual	intellectual
voice	gesture	speech
feeling	loving	thinking
to do	to be	to know
limbs (or lower trunk and legs)	trunk (or upper trunk and arms)	head
lower	middle	upper
front	side	back

excentric	normal	concentric
opposition	succession	parallelism
beauty	goodness	truth

From the trinity, Delsarte developed the "ninefold accord" in which each element of a trinity would be divided into its own triune aspects (see Illustration 5). Every trinity whether abstract or concrete could be thus subdivided.

Delsarte considered the trinitarian principle universal and fundamental, but this aspect of his theory has been the one most subject to criticism. After giving several examples of the kind of content that was organized by Delsarteans into the ninefold chart, Samuel S. Curry noted that the chief aim in such an exercise seemed to be to conform to the system without regard to the actual truth. "The greatest struggle," he wrote, "is to find nine kinds of emphasis or nine gestures or nine different attitudes such as will fit the squares." He pointed out that whether one found three or nine would be taken as a test of truth by the Delsarteans, and he, for one, rejected this aspect of the Delsarte system as artificial and mechanical (Curry 1891: 345–49). In her 1885 work, Genevieve Stebbins supported the Law of Trinity, and in fact argued for it on the basis of evidence from ancient and Asian cultures and from Swedenborg (1902: 107–12). By 1902, however, she had become sceptical of its metaphysical rationale although she still found it useful in regard to the art of expression (1902: 386–88).

In addition to his two fundamental laws, those of correspondence and trinity, Delsarte developed a number of principles on various aspects of expression. Much of this was devoted to gesture and expressive movement, and the focus here will be on this aspect of his thought. While his interest in analyzing movement is geared to realistic acting and the rendition of songs, many of his statements on movement are also relevant to the art of dance, on the one hand, and to the everyday movement of the nonprofessional, on the other. Delsarte promoted physical presence and consciousness on the part of the individual—an awareness of weight, space, rhythm, dynamics—a state in which the body has credibility and agency. Again, while the aesthetics and language differ, such an ideal is fundamental to twentieth-century acting theory and practice.

In a general statement under the heading, "On Distinction and Vulgarity of Motion," Delsarte wrote:

> Motion generally has its reaction; a projected body rebounds and it is this rebound which we call the reaction of the motion.
>
> Rebounding bodies are agreeable to the eye. Lack of elasticity in a body is disagreeable from the fact that lacking sup-

pleness, it seems as if it must, in falling, be broken, flattened or injured; in a word, must lose something of the integrality of its form. It is, therefore, the reaction of a body which proves its elasticity, and which, by this very quality, gives us a sort of pleasure in witnessing a fall, which apart from this reaction could not be other than disagreeable. Therefore, elasticity of dynamic motions is a prime necessity from the point of view of charm.

In the vulgar man there is no reaction. In the man of distinction, on the contrary, motion is of slight extent and reaction is enormous. Reaction is both slow and rapid. (*Delsarte System of Oratory* 464)

The passage illustrates Delsarte's interest in the movement qualities of the body as a whole. One wonders if he might have actually used body falls as an exercise in his teaching as was done by later American Delsarteans. The passage also demonstrates a typical Delsartean equation between quality of movement and quality of character.

Of the three agents of expression that Delsarte designated as primary—voice, gesture, and speech—he considered gesture the most basic because it "corresponds to the soul." He wrote that it is "the direct agent of the heart . . . the fit manifestation of feeling . . . the revealer of thought and the commentator upon speech . . . the spirit of which speech is merely the letter" (*Delsarte System of Oratory* 466). Without effective gesture, vocal quality and language would count for nothing, could not carry meaning on their own.

As one would expect, gesture (as all elements in his system) was subject to division and re-division. Thus he postulated a primary division of gesture into the *static*, the *dynamic*, and the *semeiotic*. He explained, "The semeiotic is its mind; the dynamic is its soul; the static is founded on the mutual equilibrium or equipoise of the agents" (*Delsarte System of Oratory* 467). In the next level of subdivision, the *semeiotic* breaks down into causes, meanings, and types and the *static* into setting, location, and direction. Of the *dynamic*, Delsarte writes:

The triple object of the dynamic are the *rhythmic, inflective* and *harmonic* forms. Dynamic rhythm is founded upon the important law of mobility [elsewhere called the Law of Velocity], inversely proportionate to the masses moved. Dynamic inflections are produced by three movements: direct movements, rotary movements and movements of flexion in the arc of a circle.

Dynamic harmony is founded on the concomitance of the relations existing between all the agents of gesture. This harmony is regulated by three states, namely: the tonic or excentric state [moving out from center], the atonic or concentric

state [moving toward center], and the normal state [centered].
(*Delsarte System of Oratory* 467–68)

Thus Delsarte theorized the components of movement in terms of (1) speed in relation to size of body or body part being moved; (2) movement line or design possibilities, given the structure of the body and its joints; and (3) spatial orientation. Of course, as recognized by Curry, there is artificiality and arbitrariness in his systematization of the components.

In a further elaboration of his movement theory, Delsarte conceived of three overall categories of motion: oppositional, parallel, and successional movement. As explained by Shawn, "*Opposition* is defined as any two parts of the body moving in opposite directions simultaneously"; *parallelism* "as two parts of the body moving simultaneously in the same direction"; and *succession* as "fluid, wavelike movement." Opposition was to be used to express force, strength, and physical or emotional power; parallelism to show weakness; and succession to depict emotion. Shawn points out the significance of successional movement in the development of modern dance (1974: 33–35). These terms held the same meaning for Delsarte and his followers as they do for us. They used the concepts in working out gesture in the narrow sense; we use them in dance composition.

Delsarte further postulated nine aspects of motion that affect expression: altitude, force, motion (the effect of emotion on the magnitude of a motion), sequence, direction, form, velocity, reaction, and extension. The Delsartean canon included a "law" concerning each aspect and how it could be used for specific meanings. For example, the Law of Altitude had to do with the positivity or negativity of assertion: the higher the gesture, the more positive; the lower, the more negative. According to the law of Motion, "excitement or passion tends to expand gesture; thought or reflection tends to contract gesture; Love or affection tends to moderate gesture." The Law of Velocity states that "velocity is in proportion to the mass moved and the force moving"; in other words, both the size of the element being moved and the nature of the emotion motivating the movement will affect the speed of motion.[1] Many of the American followers of the Delsarte system used such "laws" as a rigid and mechanical formula for expression. This does not seem to have been Delsarte's intention, however, because any "law" would have myriad manifestations, depending on all the other variables in any particular case, things such as body type, personality, setting, situation, and particularity about what was being expressed. The range of shadings and subtleties could be infinite.

Choreographers today may not be conscious of Delsarte's principles or interested in approaching composition and performance from the point of view of "laws" of motion. However, choreographers and directors of any era are, in fact, constantly working with the elements that Delsarte identified and sought to understand. Choreography classes are designed to train students to work with design (opposition, succession, parallelism), with space (altitude, direction), with time (rhythm, velocity), and with energy (force). Delsarte and his immediate followers investigated these aspects of movement in terms of dramatic or oratorical expression. Later Delsarteans and dancers developed them to revitalize the art of movement as an independent expressive art.

While Delsarte's writings contain the rationale for his system, aspects of his theory, and some descriptions of gestural patterns, very little is known about how he actually taught. As described by Mackaye, he would have students try to accomplish expression according to his ideas, but he did not really have an effective training methodology. It was the latter that Mackaye brought to the work.

MACKAYE

There is a mass of material on what Mackaye learned from Delsarte and his own interpretation and teaching of it. This includes notebooks made while he was studying with the master in France, lecture notes, brochures for his lectures and courses, lesson plans, correspondence, and published articles. Some of this is in the Dartmouth College Library and some at Louisiana State University, Baton Rouge. In addition, Stebbins' 1885 *Delsarte System of Expression* is probably a faithful rendition of Mackaye's teaching in the 1870s. In 1895, one of Mackaye's students, Marion Lowell, published a haphazard compilation of exercises and notes, *Harmonic Gymnastics and Pantomime Expression*. While she never acknowledged Mackaye in this volume, a comparison of its contents with archival materials known to be Mackaye's shows that its source was indeed his teaching.

There is nothing in Mackaye's theory or practice that contradicts the Delsarte system as known through Delsarte's writings and those of Arnaud, Delaumosne, and Giraudet. There is, however, an emphasis that distinguishes what Mackaye was presenting: his focus on what he originally called aesthetic and later harmonic gymnastics. The theoretical system thus remained the same—Mackaye taught the basic Laws of Correspondence and Trinity; the ninefold accord; the Laws of Opposition, Parallelism and Succession; and the nine Laws of Motion. He paid considerable attention, however, to practical work in physical expression, pantomime, and the "gymnastics" that would become a featured part of his own training regimen. Mackaye's innovation was not in assigning primary importance to gesture and physical expression—Delsarte had already done that—but in his development of the means whereby Delsarte's goals in this area could be realized effectively in a relatively short time.

Mackaye taught that "motion is essentially the sole means of expression," although all "motion is not necessarily expression." Comparing the raw material of motion to the plaster that might be used for a statue, he continued, "It is the element of form in motion that constitutes expression. Motion is expressive in so far as it manifests by the form it assumes the element of design and of intention."[2] This seems to imply that motion does not naturally possess form (something we would disagree with today) and that the actor or director would have to take the raw material of motion as it exists in "nature" and mold it, choreograph it, and regularize it for it to qualify as expression for performance.

Mackaye considered these principles relevant to his own specialization as well as to everyday comportment. He stated:

> What we need especially in these days of indifference to nobility bearing is a Culture which will gift us with a clear insight into the degrading influence of slovenly ways and awaken the ambition to attain to more manly and womanly modes of motion. In a word the Sciences most neglected in these days of desperate devotion to money hunting is the Science of Emotion and its Expression—and yet this Science illuminates the hidden springs of Human nature—elevates our ideals of Manhood and enables us to develop its Essence by assisting us to acquire its Manners.[3]

While Mackaye was mainly involved in professional theatre work and in training people for acting or oratory, this statement, made at a public lecture, emphasizes a characteristic of the Delsarte canon that was carried from Delsarte himself through its various developments in the United States: it was seen as a universal system, efficacious for people in all walks of life, useful in any profession or for people in no profession at all. The fundamental premise, as noted in the discussion of Delsarte above, was the correspondence between the outer manifestation of movement and the inner character and ultimate worth of the person.

Mackaye agreed with Delsarte that pantomime, or expressive motion, was the primary expressive agent and a necessary foundation for the other agents, voice and speech. How could it be otherwise when, in *nature*, one could observe that animals and infants could be very expressive without verbal language, and that, with adults, motion always seemed to precede any kind of vocal sound including speech? For the creation of *art*, however, pantomimic expression seemed to be the most difficult to perfect,[4] hence the development of Mackaye's training methods. It was unfortunate, perhaps, that they were called "gymnastics," since this confused them in some minds with exercises purely for physical training.

In 1875, Mackaye offered five courses in New York City that were to comprise a "reproduction in English" of the *Cours d'esthetique appliquée* that Delsarte had given in Paris (Mackaye 1875). Mackaye's courses (each of which met twice a week for six weeks and cost $100) were: Philosophy of Human Nature, Expression in Graphic Art, Expression in Oratory, Expression in Dramatic Art, and Aesthetic Gymnastics. In his prospectus, Mackaye subtitled the latter course The Psychologic Training of the Human Body, and wrote that it consisted of "a series of effective exercises in gesture, attitude and facial expression, created in careful obedience to the profoundest principles of grace, precision and power of expression in the human form" (1875: 12). He continued with the statement at the beginning of this chapter and claimed that the course was of value to painters, sculptors, orators, and actors—and even to "the student of moral philosophy, because it shows the powerful influence of pantomimic motion, when practically applied as a means of developing human character." Again, universal application was stressed. In the Aesthetic Gymnastics lessons, the following material was to be covered: "Nature, Aims, and Method of Aesthetic Gymnastics"; principles of and exercises in decomposing (relaxation) and recomposing motion; and "Laws of Grace and Power" applied to motion of the limbs, motion of the head, cooperation between limbs and head, motion of the torso, and cooperation of head, limbs, and torso (1875: 50–51).

In the prospectus for a later school, his School of Acting at the Lyceum Theatre, Mackaye again based his instruction on Delsarte's principles and announced a two-year course featuring a significant amount of physical training. During the first year, three out of eight courses were devoted to it: Elements of Pantomimic Expression; Harmonic Gymnastics, or Exercises for the perfection of the Pantomimic Organization of the student; and "Pantomimic Gymnastics, or Exercises in Natural Pantomime, for the purpose of developing an instinctive obedience to those laws of Nature which govern expression in the Head, Torso and Limbs." The second year included "descriptive pantomime" as distinct from "elliptic pantomime."[5] Either year the students could pay extra for optional instruction in "Dancing—historic, character and choreologic," with fencing and vocal and instrumental music (Mackaye 1885; and "Mackaye's School of Acting"). This was an innovative addition to the curriculum! It is unfortunate that we do not have some indication about what was taught in the dance course and by whom.

It was Mackaye's aesthetic gymnastics that fed into future developments in physical culture and dance, so that aspect of his work will be considered in some detail. In one of his lectures on expression in nature and art, Mackaye gave a full explanation of the principles underlying his method. His goal was to train for expression that was, at the same time, "true to nature" and "spontaneously charming in form." He equated charm with grace in motion, and taught that it was dependent on a characteristically triune set of qualities: (1) "ease—which gives repose and suavity in action"; (2) "precision—which economizes force, eliminates confusion, and gives clearness to expression"; and (3) "harmony—which secures completeness and gives potent significance to action." To achieve the goal, it would be necessary for the body to "undergo a very severe and exceptional training" with focus on three sets of principles: the Static, the Dynamic, and the Psychic. What Mackaye termed "Static Principles, or those which perfect the Pantomimic mechanism of the body," prescribed the necessity for flexibility, sufficient muscle tone to make possible a range of muscular tensions, and poise or equilibrium. The three "Dynamic Principles" that "were to perfect the Pantomimic activity of the body" were that (1) parallel movements should be successional; (2) oppositional movements should be simultaneous; and (3) in both kinds of movement, velocity should be in reverse ratio to the mass being moved. Finally, "Psychic Principles, or those which perfect the significance of pantomimic activity," concerned the order of expressional elements (face to gesture to speech), the modulation of action, and contrast.[6] These ideas are consistent with Delsarte's theory, but demonstrate an organization and emphasis that is characteristic of Mackaye's approach.

Mackaye's gymnastics were designed to develop what he considered the basics of effective expression: the trinity of poise (equilibrium), flexibility, and precision, and also what he termed the "Gamuts of Expression."[7] Poise would be promoted by exercises that worked from a standing, centered body to shifts of weight as the torso and head adjusted to create a balance. For example, the center of gravity in the standing body can be balanced on the whole foot, or it can shift forward over the toes or backward to the heels. One exercise involves just such actions; another entails a rising up on the balls of the feet. In each case, the whole body is to be balanced over where the weight rests (Lowell 13–15). The most typical of the poise exercises involves three parts of the body in balanced opposition. For example, in the simplest of these, with the feet in an opened position sideways, the weight shifts to one foot, say the right; to achieve harmonic balance, the right hip adjusts to the right, the torso to the left, and the head to the right (Lowell 9–11). Such exercises were also done on the diagonal and front to back and could involve large movements with arms and legs.

Exercises in decomposing (or relaxation) developed the second basic element, flexibility, by freeing the body. Their purpose was to "liberate all agents of Expression in the body and to . . . obliterate from the muscular fibre all the . . . automatic tendency to action that may exist in them.

... We must practice these exercises in order to get the will out. We will then be able intelligently to put will into them."[8] Mackaye believed that decomposing exercises would "develop throughout the whole organization a flexibility and pliability which are the physical basis of perfect ease" (Lowell 8). Relaxation was thus necessary to prepare the body for expression. It is interesting to compare Mackaye's ideas with those of F. Mathias Alexander and Jerzy Grotowski. Each perceived an important function of training to be that of clearing the body—of getting rid of that which impedes freedom—as a prerequisite to developing good habits of body use or effective expression (see Alexander 1990; Grotowski 1969).

Mackaye's exercises for decomposing are designated for both small and large parts of the body, including fingers, hands, arms, shoulders, head, whole torso, feet, legs, hips, and even the jaw, lips, and eyes. The techniques include simply releasing the body part (letting it drop or hang), shaking it, swinging it, and massaging it. Often one hand shakes, swings, or massages another body part to help relax it. Large decomposing movements include arm and leg swings; body bends forward, back, and to the side; and circling of the torso.[9]

Recomposing was achieved by means of all the exercises in expression that were part of the system and that were taught to promote Mackaye's third fundamental element, precision, which included grace and control. While decomposing exercises developed "conditions of ease," recomposing exercises developed "conditions of precision and harmony."[10] There are recomposing exercises for every part of the body from the smallest to the largest and for the body as a whole. They include static positions, gestures, and at least two movement activities. "Attitudes" of the torso make up the static positions. For example, a "normally erect" position denotes "fulness and repose," a contracted torso expresses repression, and a relaxed torso suggests "prostration, imbecility and indolence" (Lowell 146–56). There are gesture exercises for the hands, the arms, the head, and the torso, and for each gesture, some or all of the following are specified: the starting position of the body part in space; the type of path to be made by the gesture (straight, circular, or spiral); the direction in which the gesture moves; and the expressive meaning of the gesture. Attention is also given to transitions from one gesture to another.

There are only a few movement activities in Mackaye's exercise program. One that might be expected is walking. To express various emotional states, intentions, or character traits, the walk is varied by combining elements of rhythm, speed, body carriage, and length of stride. For example, a walk in an even, slow rhythm, with a centered carriage and short stride, would express "complete indifference, nonchalance or carelessness"; on the other hand, a walk in an even fast rhythm, with carriage forward and a long stride, would express "potent explosive vivacity" (Lowell 298–306). To prepare for walking, the students were given exercises similar to ballet *tendus* and *rond de jambes* (Lowell 18–21).

A movement exercise that is surprising to find in this context, since it is purely "gymnastic" with no emotional meaning, is entitled "Elastic Exercises of Legs." There are four movements in it: (1) hop on the ball of the left foot while throwing the right leg straight to the front; (2) leap onto the ball of the right foot (bringing it down exactly where the left one was) and, at the same time, bend the left leg "in such a way as to bring the back of the calf of the leg well up against the thigh"; (3) hop on the ball of the right foot, flinging the left leg forward; and (4) repeat motion #2 but leap onto the left foot and bend the right leg. The student is to repeat the movements "as often as possible without painful fatigue" (Lowell 178–79). This exercise is so much more vigorous than anything else associated with Mackaye's teaching that one wonders where it came from. Was it there because he had some intuitive awareness of the value of an aerobic type of conditioning to the general strength and endurance of the body?

There was strong disagreement, especially during the 1890s, about who had devised aesthetic or harmonic gymnastics—Delsarte or Mackaye. The controversy heated up during and after the visit of Marie Géraldy to the United States in February 1892. She saw the broad spectrum of elaboration that had occurred in physical culture during two decades of Delsartism in the United States and was appalled at what was being taught in her father's name. She claimed that her father had taught no gymnastics of any kind, while on the other side, William R. Alger argued that aesthetic gymnastics must have been invented and taught by the elder Delsarte since Gustave was teaching them in Paris as part of his father's training system (Alger 1894). Of course, Gustave could very well have been in the class sessions conducted jointly by Delsarte and Mackaye in 1869–1870 and learned them there. It is interesting in light of this controversy that the student notebooks and the reports of Delsarte's courses never mention a unit on aesthetic gymnastics.[11]

Whether or not Mackaye should be credited with these exercises has been confused by the fact that he minimized his own role in the development of the American Delsarte system until his later years. As he grew older and saw Delsartism grow into a broad, popular, and sometimes faddish movement, he decided to speak out and claim credit for what he perceived as basically his own system of expression. In a letter written to his wife, dated 11 April 1892, he wrote:

> *In relation to Harmonic—or as I first called them, Aesthetic Gymnastics,—they are, in philosophy as well as in form, absolutely my own alone*, though founded, in *part*, upon some of the princi-

ples formulated by Delsarte.—*In the beginning of my teaching I never dreamed of separating my work from his,* for it was done in the same spirit as his, and I cared not for the letter, nor the fame.—It is only now, when others are teaching so much nonsense in his name, and basing it upon the truths stolen from me, that I am forced to do this. (reprinted in P. Mackaye 2: 270)

The controversy was not settled in the 1890s, and it is impossible to resolve it today. In the broad history of the Delsarte system, it is not so important to know who actually invented aesthetic gymnastics. What is crucial is that they *were* created and widely disseminated. If Delsarte's original theory was the first step in the development of new possibilities in dance, these exercises provided the next step. It is likely that Mackaye did invent them, but even if he did not, he organized them, taught them, and developed them into a coherent and richly detailed system of physical training for expression.

What began to develop under Mackaye and was further elaborated by his followers is clearly distinguishable from the original system of Delsarte himself. While American proponents of the system in the late nineteenth century based their work on Delsarte's theory and identified it as "Delsartean," what developed was a greatly expanded complex of theory, training, and performance. Mackaye is a transitional figure between the system of Delsarte himself and the elaborations that would become characteristic of American Delsartism. His work led directly to that of Genevieve Stebbins.

NOTES

1. Quotations are from Stebbins 1902: 257–62; see also Shawn 1974: 47–49, who bases his discussion of these laws on Stebbins.
2. Steele Mackaye, Fourth Lecture, New York, 17 January 1877, in Delsarte Archive, Louisiana State University, Box 3, Folder 56b.
3. Steele Mackaye, "Gesture as a Language," undated lecture (probably Boston, 1874), in Delsarte Archive, Louisiana State University, Box 3, Folder 26b.
4. Steele Mackaye, undated lecture on expression in nature and art, Mackaye Archive, Dartmouth College, Box 7, Folder 7.
5. As Mackaye described these two types of pantomime, elliptic would be the subjective expressive element and descriptive the objective action. For example, if one points to the door, the pointing itself is descriptive while the manner of pointing (forcefully, off-handedly, etc.) would be elliptic.
6. Steele Mackaye, untitled and undated lecture, Mackaye Archive, Dartmouth College, Box 7, Folder 7. See also Lowell.
7. In Mackaye's system, there were three sets of "Gamuts of Expression in the Face," each with seven expressions. The performer (or student) would pass through the series "dissolving very slowly the one into the other." One of the

series consisted of the following: repose, attention, stupor, amazement, horror, terror, and madness. In addition, Mackaye conceived of a "Gamut of Emotion in Pantomime," which had 21 elements including such things as reflection, sincere affirmation, anger, and appeal for mercy. P. Mackaye 2: Appendix: xliv–xlv.

8. Undated notes, Delsarte Archive, Louisiana State University, Box 2, Folder 51.

9. Lowell 11–12, 15–18, 34–38, 77–80, 140–42, 145–46; and materials in the Delsarte Archive, Louisiana State University, and the Mackaye Archive, Dartmouth College.

10. Notes, Delsarte Archive, Louisiana State University, Box 2, Folder 51.

11. On the controversey, see Coyrière 1892; Bishop 1892a: Appendix; F. W. Adams 1892b; Woodward 1893; and "Delsartiana," May 1892 and June 1892.

Chapter 7

Genevieve Stebbins: Searching for Knowledge

> If any one were to ask me, Whom do you consider has had the greatest influence on your system of teaching, your work and your art? I would answer, Delsarte; not because I have learned more from him than from others, but because of the subtle enthusiasm his life and work have created within me. (Stebbins 1902: 397)

> It has taken me many years of study to get at the penetralia of Delsarte's system. . . . [A]nd not until the speculations of the Alexandrian school and the whole realm of metaphysics and psychology, from Spencer to Catholicism, had been explored, did I fully comprehend the viewpoint from which Delsarte observed nature and man. (Stebbins 1902: 385)

Genevieve Stebbins was never modest in making claims of erudition, but it seems indisputable that she *was* a voracious reader who delved into many areas of knowledge as she developed her approach to physical culture and expression. While her contemporaries as well as later dance historians have associated her work almost exclusively with the Delsarte system, she herself sought to establish, by means of both the titling of some of her books and the statements within them, that she had created her own unique system—that the Delsarte material was simply one of its foundations, albeit a crucially important one (see, for example, 1893: 57–58; 1902: 397, 401–407). This chapter explores some of Stebbins' delvings and considers their relationship to her work as teacher, theorist, and artist.[1] The next chapter then looks at the resulting content and methodology of her teaching.

Each of Stebbins' major publications—the 1885 *Delsarte System of Expression*, the extensive material added to it in the 1902 edition, the 1893 *Dynamic Breathing and Harmonic Gymnastics*, and *The Genevieve Stebbins System of Physical Training* of 1898 and 1913—represents a different phase or facet of her thinking and her approach to training in physical culture and expression. She reveals her theoretical interests most explicitly in *Dynamic Breathing*, in which she draws on scientific and metaphysical principles as her basis for what she calls "psychical, aesthetic, and physical culture," and in the new material in the 1902 edition of *Delsarte System of Expression*, with its emphasis on physical culture, expression, speculative thought, and the arts.[2]

Stebbins' first major work, the 1885 *Delsarte System of Expression*, is a manual presenting what she had learned of Delsartean theory and exercises from Mackaye, and in that, she suggests connections between the Delsarte canon and concepts from contemporary history, philosophy, and art theory as well as from past and present Western and non-Western cultures. Such occasional and brief references, a kind of cultivated name dropping, were characteristic of the writing of her day—authors would enhance their credibility by placing their subjects within broad historical and cultural contexts. In contrast to such pro forma contextualization, in her volumes of 1893 and 1902, Stebbins goes beyond brief references and her discussions indicate that she had seriously and critically studied many of the sources to which she was drawn.

It is interesting to note that, despite the increase in writings by women in the nineteenth century, all but one of Stebbins' sources are male. The areas that attracted her most were predominantly in the male sphere during that era: the physical and social sciences (including medicine), speculative thought, and the arts in both Western and non-Western traditions. The only woman she cites is Angélique Arnaud, one of the few contemporary sources on Delsarte and his work. In her search for knowledge, Stebbins did not limit herself to American specialists; she was also familiar with works from Great Britain, France (in French), and other European countries (in translation).

The fundamental area of knowledge for Stebbins to master was expression. Her work was based on her initial training in the Delsarte system with Mackaye and on her study of the works of Delaumosne and Arnaud, the unpublished materials given to her by Delsarte's widow, and the Delsarte materials published in later editions of *Delsarte System of Oratory*. She quoted Arnaud as early as 1885 in the first edition of *Delsarte System of Expression* and Delsarte himself in subsequent editions. Giraudet's treatise had not yet been published when she wrote her first work, but even in the 1902 edition, she only mentions his articles, not his book (445n). Occasional references and discussions scattered throughout Stebbins' publications show that she was well acquainted with the teachings and writings of other American Delsarteans such as William R. Alger, Lewis B. Monroe, and Moses True Brown, as well as with leaders in expression such as Samuel S. Curry who incorporated selected aspects of the Delsarte system into their work. However, Stebbins never mentions the writings or activities of fellow female Delsarteans such as Hovey, Bishop, and Georgen. Presumably they had nothing new to offer her; in fact, at least some of them had learned initially from her, and, for the most part, they had not developed the system any further. Stebbins, of course, also studied or consulted with non-Delsartean specialists in acting, elocution, voice, and rhetoric—figures such as Regnier on the actor's art, Oskar Guttman on voice, and Alexander Melville Bell, whose analysis of vowels and consonants she quotes in *Society Gymnastics*.

As was typical among Delsartean proponents, Stebbins was not interested in expression in the narrow context of dramatic and elocutionary training, but rather in its relation to all aspects of life and to the arts in general. For someone like Stebbins, who belonged to and worked within the elitist "cultivated" subculture of nineteenth-century America, some knowledge of the arts, art history, and aesthetics was, of course, a requirement. However, Stebbins probably dug more deeply into these subjects than many in her class or field. As an actress she would have known the contemporary and historical dramas that provided her with roles, but she also apparently became familiar with other significant playwrights and with the dramatic theory and theatrical practices of the past (see, for example, Stebbins 1886; and Stebbins 1902: 425–38). Stebbins also studied and learned about the plastic arts, dance, and literature. It is interesting, however, considering how important music has been throughout the ages as a component of dance, theater, and ritual and as a creative form in its own right, that Stebbins rarely mentions it in her writings. She apparently found no need to study music or its history; in any case she does not write about it. Stebbins did use music in some of her teaching and her performances as is mentioned in reviews of her presentations (see, for example, N. A. 1893); in vague recommendations (for a waltz or a march) in some of her drills (1913a: 84–132); and in the notation of unidentified music for seven pieces to be used for the exercises in *Society Gymnastics* (1888: 97–108). The only reference to her talking about music is found in the description of one of her classes in which she brought up music in relation to bodily harmony (Wilbor 1891: in Stebbins 1902: 481–82).

Stebbins' knowledge and veneration of the arts and literature of classical antiquity led to important components in her theory and practice. She shared with her contemporaries a belief both in the existence of absolute and eternal principles of "true art" and in classical Greek art as the most perfect embodiment of those principles (see, for example, 1902: 370–71, 419). We have seen in Chapter 4 that in 1902 Stebbins wrote of her visits to art collections in European museums in the early 1880s to check for herself the validity of Delsarte's theories against the authority of classical art. Since antique sculpture furnished what she considered ideal models, she used pictures of Greek and Roman statues to illustrate principles of expression and to teach by example. One wonders what if anything she had seen of Greek vase paintings depicting lewd satyrs and comic actors, and what she might have thought of that type of classical expression. In any case, what she understood of classical art formed the basis of her approach to the popular medium of statue posing, in which she sought to render the universal and ideal qualities that she perceived in the ancient marbles. Actually, the adherence to what she understood as classical principles of balance, repose, and universality informed all her efforts in developing both physical exercises and artistic expression.

There are many references to dance in Stebbins' writings, and she expresses great interest and respect for the art, particularly in ancient, non-Western, and ritual contexts. Her most complete discussion appears in the chapter titled "Pantomime" in the 1902 edition of *Delsarte System of Expression*, which relies heavily on a *Popular Science Monthly* article, "The Evolution of the Dance" (Vance 1892). Stebbins evaluates what the author has written, indicating a rather extensive (and sometimes inaccurate) knowledge of world dance on her own part and the likelihood that she had devoted considerable attention to it. She never mentions Lily Grove's ground-breaking 1895 volume on dance that was published in England, but reviewed in the United States as well.

Whether Stebbins' familiarity with dance came mainly from readings or the experience of seeing it is impossible to say. She criticized ballet as the worst form of the art because of its lack of expression (1902: 469), but there is no hint of how much, if any, ballet she had seen or in what contexts. Stebbins was also appalled by what were called "Oriental dances" at the Chicago World's Columbian Exposition of 1893 (1902: 471n). She must have been referring to the gyrations of the so-called Little Egypt, whose sensational shaking and shimmying reportedly shocked—and attracted—a large public (see Farrah 1993; Wayne 1993). Stebbins compared this "fraud" with a "higher and more beautiful" kind of Eastern dance that she perhaps had seen, read about, or only imagined.

Stebbins was aware that dance had been an important expressive medium in ancient Greece. She wrote:

> As an art-factor, pantomimic folk-dance cannot be overrated. Out of the old rural songs and the local cultus dances—trans-

mitted from generation to generation as mysteries and religious festivals—the marvelous structure of the Greek drama was evolved. Dionysius, the god of wine and the Bacchic revel, became, in course of time, the patron of the drama. Indeed, several of the great dramatists, as Eschylus [*sic*] and Sophocles, were clever and skillful dancers, who led in the chorus. They introduced the traditional dances in their plays for artistic purpose; while the songs sung to the accompaniment of the dance took more formal shape in that kind of poetry known as the ballad. (1902: 464)

Obviously if the ancient Greeks respected this art, and it was the foundation for the loftiest forms of drama, Stebbins would be inclined to give serious thought to dance in general, and this she did.

Outside of the arts, Stebbins pursued knowledge in what she considered related and relevant disciplines. One such discipline was the field of physical education, which had been growing and diversifying in the United States throughout the nineteenth century.[3] She investigated a broad spectrum of traditional and current ideas and practices to determine what would be of use to her own endeavors. She studied the work of prominent contemporary leaders such as Dr. Dudley A. Sargent (1849–1924) and Dr. William G. Anderson (1860–1947), both of whom had medical degrees. Such training was not unusual since the emphasis in physical education at that time was on the improvement of health and the correction of defects (Brown and Beiderhase 34). Sargent, the pioneering director of physical education at Harvard and other institutions, had made scientific studies of what worked and what did not in physical training, developed light apparatus for his gymnasiums, and promoted physical education for women as well as men (Gerber 1971: 283–301). Anderson directed the program of health and physical education at Yale University and founded and directed the Chautauqua School of Physical Education (1886–1904) and other institutions (Gerber 1971: 332–38). Both men were heavily involved in the training of teachers and the development of a professional organization, what would become the American Association for Health, Physical Education and Recreation, so their influence was widespread. Sargent and Anderson set the example by taking a nondogmatic creative approach in their search for methods to fulfill physical education goals for the entire population. To this end, they explored different kinds of physical training including the Delsarte gymnastics and various dance forms as well as the popular German Jahn and Swedish Ling gymnastics and various sports (Gerber 1971: 293–94, 335–37). Stebbins' research into the work of Sargent and Anderson gave her the most contemporary information on physical training and undoubtedly encouraged her own eclectic approach.

Of the various physical training regimens promoted in her day, the one that most interested Stebbins was the Swedish or Ling gymnastics. This had originated with Per Henrik Ling (1776–1839) and been developed further by followers, particularly his son Hjalmar Frederick Ling (1820–1886), at Sweden's Royal Gymnastics Central Institute (Gerber 1971: 155–73; Leonard 148–72). Per Henrik Ling had conceived of four interrelated branches of gymnastics: pedagogical, military, medical, and aesthetic (Gerber 1971: 157–58). The Ling medical gymnastics were introduced into the United States perhaps as early as the 1850s and the pedagogical regimen began to attain prominence in American education in the 1880s (Leonard 329).

Stebbins credited the Ling method as one of the three main foundations of her own system, along with Delsartean gymnastics and "ceremonial forms of Oriental prayer" (see below). She believed that these disciplines, "properly combined and graded into systematic progressive exercises, constitute a perfect system of gymnastics, . . . [with] all the elements essential to evolve beauty of form, graceful motion, and artistic presentation" (1902: 401).

What led Stebbins to seriously investigate the Ling system was her developing interest in the therapeutic value of exercise. She studied the Ling medical gymnastics with Dr. George H. Taylor (1821–1896), a physician and the author of such works as *An Exposition of the Swedish Movement-Cure* (1860; republished as *Health by Exercise*, 1879), *Diseases of Women* (1871), *Health for Women* (1879) and *Pelvic and Hernial Therapeutics* (1885). In the Preface to his 1860 *An Exposition of the Swedish Movement-Cure*, Taylor clearly stated his goal: to replace traditional medicine with exercise cures. He wrote: "Blessed, say I, is the man or woman who has a *good doctor*, but more blessed he *who can do without him!* To enable my reader *so to do* has been my main aim in this *manual*" (1860: ix).

In line with a small but growing number of nineteenth-century doctors and educators (see Stanley 41–55), Taylor advocated physical fitness for female children and adults as well as for males, writing:

> [T]he prevalent amount of disease among females is not a sacred birthright derived from the providential constitution of things, but . . . is *acquired*, and follows as a necessary consequence of the inharmonious action of the organism, imposed by the customs of society and the neglect of bodily culture. (1879a: 23)

Taylor backs up his views with a discussion of movement in relation to health in Asia and the classical world as well as in Western writings from the sixteenth century up to his own day, a contextualization that would certainly have appealed to Stebbins. He meticulously analyzes body chemistry in relation to movement and a range of positions and movements of all parts of the body. He describes therapeutic exercises and discusses various diseases, hygiene, the effects of heat and cold, and (briefly) mental health. His beliefs in the mind-body relationship and the power of the individual to effect his or her own state of health can be found throughout his work.

Stebbins' study with Taylor led her to the conclusion that the Delsarte and Ling methods had much in common, even though they emphasized different aspects of physical development. Ling's interest in the relationship between thought and action had its parallel in the Delsartean correspondence between body and mind. In Stebbins' opinion, the "Delsartean" statue posing could be seen as working with this relationship as well as conforming to Ling's emphasis on the value of slow sustained movement in the performance of exercise. She believed that, even though Ling had concentrated on the purely physical, he was always aware of its mental and moral implications. Delsarte, in contrast, had focused on expression without the knowledge of the physical possessed by Ling. Thus, together the two systems complemented each other (Wilbor 1892: 181). As Stebbins explained, "Delsarte has given the esthetics and Ling the athletics of a perfect method" (1902: 406). For a few months (June to September 1892) she advertised in *Werner's Voice Magazine* that what she was teaching was "Ling-Delsarte." While she did not continue to use that designation, Stebbins acknowledged what she had learned from Taylor in the Preface to her 1893 *Dynamic Breathing* (vi), and wrote of the importance of the Ling system in her 1902 *Delsarte System of Expression* (401, 406). She also added some of the Ling exercises to her own practical work.

In addition to the arts and sciences, religions of the world stimulated Stebbins' thought and her quest for a total system of what she came to call "psycho-physical" training. What Stebbins found lacking in the Delsarte-Ling combination was what she characterized in 1902 as "the breathing and the mental imagery which have been the common property of every mystic and occult fraternity under the sun" (1902: 406). This constituted the third element of her system: "The ceremonial forms of Oriental prayer" (1902: 401). In *Dynamic Breathing*, she refers to dance in relation to this element:

> The system of psycho-physical culture and the various exercises for the same given in this work are based chiefly [on Delsarte and Ling] combined with others more occult and mystic in their nature, which have been taken from those ideal and charmingly beautiful motions of sacred dance and prayer practiced by various oriental nations for certain religious and metaphysical effects, while the whole is blended with a

system of vital dynamic breathing and mental imagery.
(1893: 59)

While the "occult and mystic" elements are undoubtedly embodied in
many of her general exercises, some are identified specifically, such as
"yoga breathing," "salaam," and "dervish exercise" in *Dynamic Breathing*
and the "Eastern Temple Drill" in *The Genevieve Stebbins System of Physical Training.*

As Stebbins was developing her system, breathing became more and
more fundamental to it. In the original text of *Delsarte System of Expression*, she mentions it only in her section on the voice (1902: 287–88),
quoting a brief passage from Delsarte and referring the reader to *Gymnastics of the Voice* by the German dramatic reader and teacher Oskar
Guttman (1822–1889); and in *Society Gymnastics*, she writes only a bit
more (73–75). In *Dynamic Breathing*, however, she goes deeply into its
theory and practice. She also includes more breathing exercises and pays
more attention to breathing in other exercises than she had in her earlier
works.

In *Dynamic Breathing* Stebbins draws on knowledge from the fields of
the arts, sciences, physical education, and religion to help her understand
the process and significance of breathing and to lend authority to her
arguments. In her Preface, Stebbins credits Regnier, with whom she had
studied in 1881, for lessons on "dynamic nerve-energy in the voice, and
his many artistic suggestions"; Dr. George H. Taylor for teaching her the
Ling medical gymnastics; Dr. J. R. Buchanan, an "eclectic" physician,
who had helped her with anthropology and other studies[4]; and Dr. Dudley Sargent for introducing her to various approaches to exercise. In first
place, however, she thanks, without identifying, "a friend, an analytical
thinker and traveler, who has been our Collaborateur throughout" (vi).
Would this have been her husband Norman Astley? Or, perhaps,
Thomas Burgoyne? Or someone else she knew through the Brotherhood
of Light? She clearly did not want that known.

Stebbins projected *Dynamic Breathing* as the complete outline of her
teachings and "the real principles, both metaphysical and vital upon
which they are based" (v). To present this work in the broadest possible
context, Stebbins opens with a discussion of the nature of the universe
and its human inhabitants. In Chapter 1, "The Breath of Life," she addresses what she calls "the present contest between religion and science"
(2) as a way of understanding reality, and it is clear that her intention is
to resolve that conflict in the course of the book. Stebbins begins her
argument with evidence from science. She identifies the "living breath"
as the "life principle" and relates it to solar energy, drawing on the ideas
of the astronomer Sir John Herschel (1792–1871) and the physicist John
Tyndall (1820–1893) (5–10). Stebbins uses statements from Herschel's

1849 *Outlines of Astronomy* and Tyndall's 1862 *Heat Considered as a Mode of Motion* to establish that the sun is the source of all energy and movement, in short, everything on the earth—noting that what for Herschel had been speculation was by the time of Tyndall "the impregnable facts of exact science" (7). Tyndall's claim that there are invisible as well as visible rays emanating from the sun leads Stebbins to speculate on the relationship (or "correspondence") between the visible and nonvisible.

After establishing her scientific foundation, Stebbins addresses what she considered to be the more lofty realms of speculative thought:

> We must now bring to our aid the powers of the imagination to follow out metaphysically the same line of truth, and transfer the same laws to a higher plane of action. In doing this, we shall not leave the safe realm of verity and fact. We shall simply appeal, ... to the now almost universal acknowledgement of the existence of the psychic principle in humanity, of the soul, in fact, and its wonderful powers over mind and matter as seen in the phenomena of Hypnotism, Mental Healing, and Telepathy. (1893: 11)

Her conclusion is that

> everything in nature is composed of body and soul; the former, in the terms of matter, gives motion; and the latter, in the terms of spirit, gives mind and sensation. The bioplasm of the one and the psychoplasm of the other constitute the primordial life—the base of all higher forms of existence. (1893: 11)

This universal principle forms the basis of her conclusions in this book. In subsequent chapters, she discusses the relationship between breathing and mental/emotional states, brain function, and imagination. It is interesting to note that despite Stebbins' and the other Delsarteans' attachment to the idea of correspondence between the physical and the mental/spiritual, they were firmly rooted in the belief that there is a "higher" and "lower" order of experience and consciousness.

In building her arguments in *Dynamic Breathing*, Stebbins draws on her own imagination and intuition and on sources ranging from art criticism to metaphysics, from religious history to treatises on hallucination. She quotes from the ever popular John Ruskin, for example: "[T]he first function of the imagination is the apprehension of ultimate truth" (32). She turns to George Henry Lewes for a distinction between "the mental image of creative thought or memory and the mental picture we obtain from physical vision" (34). She discusses the theories of several doctors on hallucinations (35–37) and the metaphysical concepts of Hinduism,

Buddhism, Islam, and Christianity (42–45). Such passages demonstrate Stebbins' fascination with the relationship of the mind and spirit to the body and to the concept of mind-body relationship embodied in Delsarte's Law of Correspondence. Finally she leads the reader into exercises for breathing, relaxation, energizing, and physical culture. These, which will be discussed in the next chapter, include elements from Delsarte-Mackaye, Ling (through Taylor), other contemporary exercise regimes, and Eastern meditational forms.

The pages of *Delsarte System of Expression* also demonstrate Stebbins' interest in religious and philosophical literature. For example, in discussing William R. Alger's statement that "the Delsarte philosophy is simply an esthetic translation of the scholastic philosophy," she claims to have spent three years in daily study of the early Christian writings of Origen, Tertullian, St. Jerome, St. Augustine, and St. Basil, as well as those of the thirteenth-century theolgian St. Thomas of Aquinas (392–93) Could that have been true? Are such statements exaggerations—made to show off her erudition? Or, do they reflect actual practice, stimulated by a mind truly obsessed with knowledge, with curiosity about almost everything? We will never know, but it seems clear that Stebbins was intensely interested in religious thought whether it came from Christian or Eastern sources, from antiquity or modern occultism. It provided another key to the mind-body relationship that so fascinated her. Stebbins' words on religion and metaphysics also illustrate her unorthodoxy. Far from demonstrating allegiance to a particular faith—say, Christianity, the religion of most in her class and profession—her writings show a woman passionately interested in all religious thought and speculation.

Stebbins never mentions the Brotherhood of Light in any of her writings, but she was apparently involved in this occult tradition for some time before 1893, prior to writing *Dynamic Breathing* and her marriage to Astley. Occult groups such as the Brotherhood tended toward secrecy, so one would not expect Stebbins to be quoting its lessons or referring to it. Knowing, however, her connection with the Brotherhood helps to explain her more esoteric and speculative writing—particularly that of *Dynamic Breathing* with its pervasive mystical cast.

While Stebbins' ideas could have come from elsewhere, the parallels between some of her statements and the principles put forth in Hermetic Brotherhood of Luxor documents (as compiled by Godwin) or in the Church of Light brochure (in a July 1995 version, but reflecting long-held beliefs) are striking. Let us consider three examples. First, Stebbins' denial of the notion of conflict between science and religion and her reliance on both to develop her thought as well as her emphasis on "nature" are echoed in this passage from the brochure:

> There cannot be two orders of truth in the universe. Therefore, we deny that there is any antagonism between true Science

and true Religion. We accept one book as infallible in inter-
preting the Will of Deity and that is the *book of nature*. We
worship but one religion, which is also a science. It is *nature's
laws*.

In another example, Stebbins writes that "the All of human existence"
comes from the air we breathe. She elaborates:

> the physical energy so necessary for the functional existence
> of the body, the invisible dynamic forces to stimulate the
> mind, and those finer but imperceptible ethereal forces that
> nourish and expand the spiritual energies of the soul,—every-
> thing and all, [is] the outcome of that mysterious yet universal
> essence, the BREATH OF LIFE. (1893: 12)

There is a notable congruence between this second example and the following quotation from the H. B. of L. document, "The Mysteries of
Eros":

> There are two results of breathing—the first is from the in-
> spiration of common atmosphere which sustains the life of
> matter—sensation. The second result is from the inspiration
> of the magnetic, electric, more ethereal particles of the air
> which support the life of soul and emotion; that higher, inner,
> deeper part of man which concerns itself about infinite and
> eternal interests.[5] (in Godwin et al. 1995: 227)

Earlier, in *Dynamic Breathing* she almost quotes part of this passage:
"[T]he air we breathe is charged with nature's finer and more ethereal
essences—magnetism, electricity and the celestial ether" (1893: 9).

As a third example, agreement is obvious between Stebbins and the
H. B. of L. in their emphasis on the sun as the primary source of all life.
In their study of the Brotherhood's history and beliefs, Joscelyn Godwin
and his co-authors state, "[I]n the cosmogony of [Thomas Burgoyne's]
The Light of Egypt, the origin of all things lies in the primordial, divine
Central Sun that centrifugally spun off and generated the universe of
creation" (1995: 51; see also Burgoyne 1889: 6–7; and Burgoyne 1900:
168). We have seen that Stebbins draws on scientific writings to establish
that the sun is the source of everything (1893: 5–11). She goes further,
however, stating:

> The glorious central sun of our solar system, that rays forth
> his electrical life for the sustenance of his magnificent family
> of worlds is, in his material expression and law, but the ex-
> ternal visible covering for the grander ethereal, let us say spir-
> itual sun which forms those infinite spheres of light, life and

love from which the diviner part of man receives his power, from which the soul receives its inspirations and support, from which we receive the reality of life. (1893: 7)

Even with all the evidence that Stebbins had studied and to some extent accepted Brotherhood of Light doctrine, it still seems unlikely that she believed exclusively in these tenets to the exclusion of any other religious points of view. Her writings show a broad and multicultural interest in religion and philosophy. Nowhere is her eclecticism more apparent than in *The Quest of the Spirit*, a work edited rather than written by Stebbins, but with which she claims to be in total agreement (1913b: 7). This work surveys an international array of approaches to understanding life and the universe but pledges allegiance to none.

Genevieve Stebbins' quest for knowledge led her in many directions. From the core of her work in theater and her study of the Delsarte system, she branched out into various theoretical and practical studies and spent her life trying to make sense of the correspondence between the physical, on the one hand, and the mental, emotional, and spiritual, on the other. To her credit, she never lost sight of either aspect and worked against the mind/body dualism so prominent in much of Western thought. These intellectual searchings informed the practical work that Stebbins achieved in her development of training and performance. The resulting approaches to training will be discussed in the next chapter.

NOTES

1. In her writings, Stebbins mentions, quotes, or discusses the ideas of over 100 artists, thinkers, and scientists whose work she found relevant to her own quest. This material is discussed in my 1988 article, "The Intellectual World of Genevieve Stebbins," some of which is reproduced here.

2. Stebbins' *Society Gymnastics* and *The Genevieve Stebbins System of Physical Training* have only a few references to Stebbins' sources. *Genevieve Stebbins Drills* has none.

3. For information on the history of physical education, see: Ainsworth 1930; Brown and Sommer 1969; Lee 1983; Leonard 1927; Stanley 1996; Van Dalen et al. 1953; Welch and Lerch 1981.

4. Dr. Joseph Rodes Buchanan (1814–1899) identified himself on the title page of his 1893 *Manual of Psychometry* as "Professor of Physiology and Institutes of Medicine in four medical colleges successively, from 1845 to 1881—and for five years Dean of the Eclectic Medical Institute, the parent school of American Medical Eclecticism—Discoverer of the impressibility of the brain—of Psychometry and of Sarcognomy." In addition to writing on medical subjects, Buchanan also published works on anthropology and education.

5. "The Mysteries of Eros" was a compilation of practical instructions for H. B. of L. members. According to Godwin and his co-authors, Burgoyne had put

it together in 1886 or 1887 while he was residing in Denver, Colorado, and it was eventually published there as a 52-page pamphlet by Dr. Henry Wagner, a member of the H. B. of L. The text, published in Godwin et al., was acquired by Harvard University in 1929 (1995: 39, 213). It deals with good and bad aspects of sexuality as its title implies and promotes what H. B. of L. believed was the "highest," most spiritually beneficial manifestation of sexual activity and experience (in Godwin et al. 1995: 217–78).

dents Stebbins served is indicated in The New York School of Expression brochure of 1893. It states that the primary purpose of the school is "the practical training of teachers to teach Elocution and Physical Culture" (6) and emphasizes that its focus is "real work in the various branches of Expression, which command an immediate market value" (7). However, as an alternative it suggests that those students who do not seek professional training, "but who desire to study the higher and more ideal artistic branches of Expression for their Aesthetic value in personal accomplishments, can enter the private classes of Genevieve Stebbins where physical beauty and graceful deportment are the chief objects of culture" (7). Private instruction was also offered for those preparing to perform publicly in addition to, or instead of, teaching (16–17).

Unfortunately, there is little written about Stebbins' actual work in the classroom (one such report will be discussed at the end of this chapter). Her publications, however, were designed as teaching manuals, so they give a full picture of her pedagogical goals and methodology. These "how-to" books describe exercises and suggest teaching and study practices that developed out of Stebbins' evolving practical, theoretical, and philosophical interests. Along with her thinking, her exercise prescriptions changed over the years. That development can be traced by comparing the material in *Delsarte System of Expression* with that of her other works—*Society Gymnastics* (1888), *Dynamic Breathing and Harmonic Gymnastics* (1893), and *The Genevieve Stebbins System of Physical Training* (1898). We will see that from 1885 to 1898, as Stebbins learned about current physical education pedagogy, the Ling medical gymnastics, and Middle Eastern and Asian religious practices, her training regimen became more physically demanding, dealt with the body in greater totality (i.e., it did not omit mention of, nor attention to, particular body areas), and placed more emphasis on breathing. While Stebbins' teaching also included the principles she took from Delsarte and other sources (discussed in Chapter 7) and performance forms such as statue posing and drills (see Chapter 9), this chapter focuses on the actual exercise material she promoted and how it changed over time.

Genevieve Stebbins was the first in a long line of Americans to publish a teaching manual on the Delsarte system. While she reportedly traveled to France to conduct research for this, her first text, the 1885 *Delsarte System of Expression* is clearly based on what she had learned from Mackaye (all references will be to its 1902 edition). She emphasizes decomposing (relaxation) and poise (equilibrium), two of his major concepts, and in addition, her early exercises for various parts of the body and her "gamuts of expression" derived largely from him. The work consists of 21 lessons on various aspects of theory and practice. The first five lessons are written as if Stebbins is teaching a single student and reacting to her responses to the material. Each of these lessons is devoted to one aspect of the system (decomposing, harmonic poise, principle of trinity, the legs, and the walk) and includes an "aesthetic talk," followed by instruction in the exercises with interspersed commentary. Lessons 6 to 21 are written in the guise of a correspondence course and cover work with the hand, arm, torso, head, eye, facial profile, lips and jaw, Delsarte's Nine Laws of Motion, expression in pantomime, the voice, and color. In these lessons the "aesthetic talks" are eliminated and the commentary is considerably reduced.

In the 21 lessons of the *Delsarte System*, Stebbins' aesthetic gymnastics are very close to those of Mackaye. Her relaxation exercises only differ in that she places somewhat less emphasis on facial parts and adds one completely new element—a fall, in which the total body relaxes and drops to the floor. Her brief written instruction for this sounds recklessly dangerous: "Standing with your weight on back leg, bend that knee; also bend torso forward. The head should fall back. Withdraw the will from the back leg; the body will drop to the ground" (1902: 86). In her section on "Walking," Stebbins describes a back fall and a front fall that she categorizes (along with a number of nonfalling movements!) as "stage falls" (9, 165). Teaching falls makes sense in the training of actors since scripts often call for a character to collapse in one way or another. We have seen a slight indication that Delsarte might have incorporated falling into his practical work, and there is no doubt that Henrietta Hovey taught them, although in the physical culture rather than dramatic context.

Stebbins' teaching of "harmonic poise" was basically the same as Mackaye's. It will be recalled that in harmonic poise, if the weight is on the right leg, the hip is shifted toward that leg, the torso away from it, and the head toward it, thus creating a curved line. Stebbins writes that "this opposition of the three parts of the body is one of the most beautiful things I know of" and that the lines thus created "indicate a moral poise" as well as the physical. She claims that all classical statues, no matter who or what is being depicted, have this quality—the three body parts in opposition (94, 458). She urged her students to practice these assiduously in front of the mirror (83). The students were thus encouraged to develop an objective, evaluative view of what they were doing rather than relying on the subjective experience of their bodies. In the Delsartean canon, of course, if they achieved the outer form of the position or movement, it was assumed that this would both reflect and effect their "inner" selves.

In Chapter 5 of *Delsarte System*, Stebbins takes her imaginary pupil outdoors for a lesson on walking (155–64). After critiquing the pupil's defects, Stebbins explains that how someone walks indicates "habits, character and emotions" (155). After describing the "perfect" basic walk as one characterized by steps in a straight forward direction, harmonic poise with each shift of weight, and movement from the thigh, Stebbins explains how various changes from the basic walk express different temperaments or passing emotions (159). She coaches her imaginary student in various ways of walking and then suggests that they run a race together. This gives her the opportunity to point out to the student that "like all women, you roll instead of run," and then to instruct her in a properly balanced run (164–65). The exercises that follow this excursion include the above-mentioned falls, kneeling, bowing, sitting, rising from each of those descents, pivoting on two feet, and the Mackaye exercise that seems to be purely for development of strength in the calves— slowly rising onto the balls of the feet and sinking down (the ballet *élevé*) (165–68). That is an unusual exercise in this context, however, because the focus is otherwise on the quality of the movement in terms of expression and gracefulness rather than on any kind of physical conditioning of the body. At this point, it seems that Stebbins was unaware of the relationship between physical conditioning and a person's ability to achieve the kind of bodily expression she promoted.

Stebbins' developing goals in teaching and an expanded repertoire of physical exercises began to appear in print as early as 1888 in her *Society Gymnastics and Voice Culture, Adapted from the Delsarte System*. While many of the exercises, attitudes, and "laws of motion" in this volume parallel those of *Delsarte System*, there is greater focus and clarity here as well as new material. In a question and answer section at the end of the Introduction, Stebbins characterizes the body "as an instrument" and the purpose of the training, she writes, is "to free our souls by freeing the channels of communication, and to enable us to outwardly express that which is most pleasing and beautiful within" (1888: 12). There is, of course, the assumption that if "souls" are freed, only what is "pleasing and beautiful" will emerge. Stebbins, along with her contemporaries, worked within a very strict code as to what was appropriate to express.

Stebbins includes in *Society Gymnastics* some new torso, arm, and vocal work and eight breathing exercises as preparation for using the voice. She advises the teacher on the most effective order of the exercise material and recommends that the students be required to memorize every "line" in the book and be tested on it because "one cannot expect a good physical result without a clear mental comprehension of the exercises" (95). At the end of the volume, she includes seven musical scores designated as accompaniment for specific lessons (97–108).

By the time she was writing her 1893 *Dynamic Breathing and Harmonic Gymnastics*, Stebbins had become convinced that breathing was the most fundamental element in life and she placed it at the center of the training regimen she was now calling "psycho-physical culture." She defined this new term as a completely rounded system for the development of body, brain and soul; a system of training which shall bring this grand trinity of the human microcosm into one continuous, interacting unison, so that nothing shall be useless, nothing thoughtless, and consequently, nothing that is vital wasted. (1893: 57)

She later wrote that psycho-physical culture "is the perfect unison of harmonic gymnastics and dynamic breathing, during the formulation of noble ideas in the mind" (66). It seems that she was striving toward a state in which all aspects of the person would be united and functioning without conflicts and disjunctions.

The practical work in *Dynamic Breathing* is divided into four sections: breathing, relaxation, energizing, and physical culture. Most of the re-laxation exercises are the same as those in her earlier works except for two that are done lying on the floor. The other three categories, however, contain much that is new in Stebbins' system, including many specific exercises taken from the Ling medical gymnastics. This new work will be discussed in some detail.

The breathing exercises (1893: 82–90) differ considerably from those in *Society Gymnastics*. They are not simply preparation for vocal expression, but have become integral elements in the overall experience and training of the body. Seven are done standing and three lying down. Inhalation and exhalation are through the nose and the student is to feel the impact of the breath through the chest, lower back, and abdomen—and in some cases, into other areas of the body as well. The basic exercise of the series is "rhythmic breathing," in which the inhalation and exhalation are of equal duration (four heartbeats each), separated by a two-heartbeat pause between each action. The second exercise, "deep rhythmic breathing," is the same, but with the length of time devoted to each part increased. Stebbins writes that this exercise "generates a large quantity of vital energy" (1893: 82). Her basic conception of breathing parallels that of the Hermetic Brotherhood of Luxor. In "The Mysteries of Eros," for example, it is stated that slow and regular breathing results in "a gain of vitality, therefore, physical life" and that "to obtain a more har-monious influence, the heaving of the chest should be regular and its inspirations and expirations of equal duration" (in Godwin et al. 1995: 228).

Other exercises in this section include "dispersive breathing," or rhythmic breathing with the mental image of dispersing "blood and en-ergy from the brain downward to the feet" (1893: 85–86); "yoga breathing," in which the student imagines the breath surging into and out of one and another part of the body (1893: 86–87); and the "packing

breath," filling the lungs with little inhalations until full and then ex-
haling in one long flow (1893: 87). These five exercises are described
basically in physical terms with the mind focusing on what the body is
to do. In contrast, the next two involve more metaphysical mental instructions along with some body movement.

In "inspirational breathing," the breathing is accompanied by lifting
the arms and head forward to overhead and then lowering them while
the student imagines that "the powers of Divine Providence" are being
drawn in and let out with the breath. In "aspirational breathing," the
arms circle from the side to over the head where the palms meet and
then are lowered down in front of the face (prayer position) and finally
back down to the beginning position, hanging at the sides of the body.
Stebbins writes: "The mental idea for this exercise is that of aspiring for
Divine illumination and power, which exalts the whole being. The imagination responds by feeling the spiritual influx of joyous inspiration"
(1893: 89). The entire description of "aspirational breathing" is quoted
in Volume 2 of *The Light of Egypt*, which was attributed to Thomas H.
Burgoyne although it was published after his death (Burgoyne 1969: 175).
This is just one of the connections that keep appearing between Stebbins
and the Hermetic Brotherhood of Luxor.

The final three exercises in this section again focus on the physical:
"double respiration" involves mechanically working the chest muscles
as if breathing but actually holding an inhalation; "therapeutic breathing
for women" directs the breath to the pelvic area while the woman
presses with her index finger at the region of the ovaries; and "anti-
dyspeptic respiration" concentrates perception of the breath low into the
abdomen, holding the inhalation while one hand slaps the stomach for
10 to 30 seconds. These exercises demonstrate Stebbins' effort to give her
students a more intense physical experience than would have been possible from the work in her first two books or in that of much other
nineteenth-century physical culture literature. Moreover, it is significant
that Stebbins does not shy away from mentioning any body part. In both
the "yoga breathing," and the "therapeutic breathing for women," attention is directed to the abdominal and pelvic areas. In thus dealing
with the whole body, including its sexual organs, Stebbins was following
a practice that was already common in medical literature of the day (see,
for example, works by Austin; Buchanan; Kellogg; and Taylor).

The chapter on energizing begins with a new series of exercises that
Stebbins recommends to increase "personal magnetic power" as well as
"vital strength" (1893: 97). They include one and then another part of
the body separately being gradually tensed ("energized"), held, and then
released; next, the whole body is extended vertically with full tension,
held, and released; and finally, tension is used to propel the body into
an oblique lunge, which is also held and then released. Each exercise is

coordinated with inhalation, holding of the breath, and exhalation—what Stebbins terms "dynamic breathing" (1893: 98–101).

The second group of energizing exercises, Stebbins points out, "are purely aesthetic, giving a graceful control of the body" (1893: 97) and are to be done with normal as opposed to "dynamic" breathing (102). They include the harmonic poise, oppositions, and spiral successional movement, which had already appeared in her previous writings. However, there are some interesting additions such as the "spiral sway," which is to be done with "a semi-circular, rhythmic dance-motion" (1893: 105); the "spiral flight," which, "when well produced, gives a superb exercise in dance motion, as performed by many gypsy and oriental dancers" (1893: 105); and the "salaam," which she writes "is taken from the formula of Mahomedan prayer as practiced in the mosques" (1893: 106). She thus illustrates her interest in non-Western practices and her leanings toward dance, both of which can be found throughout her writings.

The chapter on energizing also includes some general observations about the exercise material, the use of the various parts of the body, and the correspondence between emotions and the body (1893: 113–16). A point that Stebbins stresses in regard to the latter is the reciprocal nature of the elements of correspondence, the outer and the inner. She writes that not only do mental states affect bodily expression, but conversely, a change in body carriage or use also affects thought process, sensations, and emotions (1893: 117). In *The Genevieve Stebbins System of Physical Training*, she comes back to this principle, claiming that "signs of expression tend through reflex action to produce states of mind" (12). As discussed in Chapter 6, this concept was a principle of Delsarte's as well as American Delsartean theory and has continued as a premise in twentieth-century acting theory. The chapter on energizing concludes with sections on "The Principles of Gesture" (1893: 116–21) and "Dynamic Walking" (1893: 121–22).

Many of the physical culture exercises that Stebbins recommends for their "special hygienic value" (1893: 123) come from the Ling regimen and appear here for the first time in her writings. She gives exercises for rotating the torso, arm, leg, and foot; vibrating a part of the body; swinging arms and legs; lifting a part of the body; and stretching (1893: 123–33). As in the relaxation, breathing, and energizing work, some of these exercises are also done lying on the floor. Some are more physically demanding than anything Stebbins has taught previously. For example, from a prone position the student is to lift her hips and hold them high with the weight balanced on toes and elbows. A similar exercise is done lying on the side with the weight balanced on one elbow and the feet (1893: 131). Both of these are examples of work taken directly from Taylor (see 1860: 220–21). Other floor exercises include double leg lifts and sit-ups from a supine position (1893: 131–32). The floor work in this section as well as in the other chapters is absolutely new to Stebbins' work. It provides bodily experiences for the students that were more intense and specific—and difficult—than anything the women had known from previous activities. It also presages the floor work that would become so important in twentieth-century modern dance.

Stebbins closes her section on physical culture exercises with recommendations regarding the use of exercise props such as Indian clubs, dumbbells, and skipping ropes to enhance muscular development (she favors them); and what clothing should be worn. She recommends, in contrast to the constricting fashionable dress of the day, "a system of dress that shall enable any woman or girl to perform every exercise given in this work without change of costume" (1893: 134). Her suggestion that there should be no need to wear special clothing for gymnastic exercise underscores the fact that, while the exercise material in this volume is more demanding than that of her first two works, it is hardly vigorous enough to cause sweating and the need to change clothes. Stebbins' work seems to be in line with a general belief of the nineteenth century that women should not exert themselves too much. Moreover, it probably would not have been considered ladylike to work up a sweat.

Stebbins' next teaching manual, *The Genevieve Stebbins System of Physical Training*, was first published in 1898. The "enlarged edition" of 1913 is exactly the same as the original except for the deletion of one acknowledgment in the beginning and the addition of one drill near the end. The work consists of three parts: Part I is mostly familiar Stebbins' material on poise, breathing, relaxation, and energizing; Part II consists of 27 series of exercises for use in schoolrooms with stationary desks (a total of 110 exercises); and Part III includes instructions for nine performance pieces called "drills" (see Chapter 9). In her Foreword, Stebbins claims that the exercises in Part I "are an epitome of all psychological physical culture" and if practiced daily will transform a person's life "into a healthy and happy one." Here, she credits her sources as her years of experience teaching physical culture, her study of the art works of antiquity, and her knowledge of "medical gymnastics" (1913a: 5). In explanatory material in the first section, she also occasionally refers to one or another authority to make a point, but there is no mention of Delsarte in this volume. Nevertheless, the exercises are simply a further elaboration of what she had been developing throughout her career. Some significant additions to the exercise repertoire are included. While she had previously recommended rising on the balls of the feet (the ballet *élevé*) and then lowering the heels, in this section on poise, she asks the student to bend and straighten the knees (*plié*) while staying in the *élevé* position (1913a: 19). This is a more difficult action in terms of both muscle strength and balance and one that requires conscious control of the abdomen and pelvic area. The breathing section now includes exercises designated for curing a headache (1913a: 30–31), invigorating the ovaries (1913a: 31–32), invigorating the lungs and preventing consumption (1913a: 32), and giving "nerve-power" (1913a: 32).

Part I ends with a "Special Drill for Home Use" that includes, in addition to the familiar material, several floor exercises that are new. They each start from a kneeling position. In the first one, the student lowers the trunk until the chin is on the floor; places the arms next to the body with the hands, palms up, toward the feet; and then, breathes while expanding the waist (1913a: 42). In this position and in variations of it in other exercises in this section, the awareness of the body again focuses on the pelvic area; it feels like the breath itself is moving all the way down the body because of the reaction of the muscles to the breath expanding the lungs. In this, as in other exercises, Stebbins is providing physical attention to and experience of parts of the body that "nice" ladies of Stebbins' class probably did not normally even dare mention or even think about except perhaps in medical terms. Was this transgressive? There is no indication of qualms on the part of Stebbins or censure on the part of those who admired her and wrote about her. Another exercise that might also have been unusual in the experience of "proper" middle-class women is that of being on their hands and knees and stretching their backs "like a dog stretching after a nap" (1913a: 43). I wonder if such activities were great fun for these ladies (there would have been no men present) or if they were somewhat embarrassing. We can see that by at least the end of the century, Stebbins was giving her students work that pushed into the consciousness physical sensations that might have been previously unfamiliar or at least ignored. While much of Stebbins' training still focused on the periphery—the outer appearance of movement—some of it was probing more deeply.

The "Schoolroom Gymnastics," which make up a large part of this work, include the familiar Stebbins' repertoire of relaxation, poise, and energizing exercises, but also more mechanical kinds of drills such as marching with the arms in various positions (1913a: 51–52) and different kinds of walks and step patterns (1913a: 52–54, 66–67, 79–81). Some of the latter she termed "Fancy Step Marching." The Stebbins recommended order of exercising for each work session: was breathing, legs, arms, trunk, head, marching, and then again, breathing (1913a: 47), an exact parallel to the order recommended in the Ling medical gymnastics (Taylor 1860: 138). The inclusion of marching and running (what we recognize as aerobic exercise) shows that by this time Stebbins recognized the value of a sustained and vigorous working of the body, at least for children. She does not state, however, her reasons for including this kind of work. It may have simply been to use up excess energy so the children would be ready to settle down and study again. Of all of Stebbins' exercise materials, these gymnastics seem the least gendered, and I wonder if she had in mind that they might be used for boys as well as girls.

Part III of *Genevieve Stebbins System of Physical Training* includes the nine drills mentioned above. While these were used as training exercises, they were particularly designed for performance—and especially for the commencement exercises of the New York School of Expression (82). The new material that was published in the 1902 sixth edition of *Delsarte System* included a bit of additional work for the voice; Delsarte's address before the Philotechnic Society of Paris; and an entirely new section, "Theory and Practice of Delsarte's System: Pantomime, Physical Culture, and Statue-posing" (with chapters numbered 1 to 12); and 32 photographs of classical statues scattered throughout the book. Most of this is theoretical or explanatory, but Chapter 11, "Hints for Artistic Statue-Posing," provides information on how Stebbins trained her students for this genre and what she considered important for their mastery of it. As stated at the beginning of this chapter, both the drills and the statue posing will be discussed in Chapter 9.

A few clues to Stebbins' classroom practice are given in an article by Elsie M. Wilbor, a frequent writer and editor for Werner's publications (Wilbor 1891: 29–31). She discusses four classes: a group of 5- to 12-year-olds in a school for the daughters of society families; the "weekly drill" of 18-year-old girls preparing to graduate from a "young ladies' seminary"; a "philosophical class" of middle-aged, wealthy ladies, held in one of their drawing rooms; and a class in "nerve-gymnastics," held in a Fifth Avenue home (Wilbor 1891). All four lessons included exercises, and those for the three older groups also featured lecture material. There is little evidence that any of the students were given vigorous or rigorous exercise. Stebbins wore regular street clothes for at least three of the sessions, loosened a bit to allow freedom of motion; and except for the older girls, who had designed a gymnastic costume for such activity, the pupils seemed to be in everyday clothing. Wilbor describes Stebbins as a striking figure who commanded attention in each setting.

Stebbins used music, at least in the children's class, and Wilbor praises the pianist for her rendering of pieces by composers such as Schubert, Liszt, Schumann, and Rubenstein. "It is played," she writes, "to assist the pupils to keep the rhythm in drilling, and partly as an inspiration to Mrs. Thompson [Stebbins]. The effect of dreamy music in the gentler, more insinuating movements, and of heroic strains in the moments of agressive action is impressive alike to teacher and pupil" (Wilbor 1891: 31).

Stebbins began the children's class by teaching them a flowing arm movement; they were to imagine that their arms and hands were tree limbs with leaves being blown by the wind. She also gave the children exercises for other parts of the body, attitudes, and oppositions. In her description of the other three classes, Wilbor is, unfortunately far more interested in what Stebbins said in the lecture components than in what she had the class do as activities. The graduating class of the young ladies' seminary worked on relaxation for "a few minutes," then sat to listen to theory. After the lecture, they did leg, arm, and head movements; oppositions; and attitudes. Wilbor writes that Stebbins did "not spare herself, but [went] through every movement as enthusiastically and carefully as if she, too, were a student" (1891: 30).

The two classes of middle-aged women consisted of more lecture than activity. In the "philosophical class," Stebbins spoke on "the music of motion," focusing more on motion than on music. To give a physical experience that would underscore her final point about the relationship of the mind and the body, Stebbins had the ladies do the "Yoga Breathing-Exercise" that was later described in *Dynamic Breathing*. Wilbor characterizes the women in the "Nerve-Gymnastics" class as needing vigorous exercise but more concerned with cultivating their brains. Stebbins lectured them on the importance of the body and its relationship to the brain and "coaxed the class into the mood of exercising" (1891: 31). She managed to give them a few exercises for various parts of the body and some instruction in breathing and oppositions. Thus Stebbins and her cohorts on the society circuit sometimes had to coddle their patrons for the advantages (financial or otherwise) that they could bring.

Stebbins' reputation, however, did not depend on her teaching in fashionable drawing rooms as much as did Henrietta Hovey's and that of some of the other Delsarteans. Stebbins enjoyed the appreciation of students of many kinds, the gratification of spreading the word (and the bodily activity) of something she thoroughly believed in, and the stimulation of providing professional training for prospective performers and teachers. Her books served to instruct many who could not study with her in person and influenced others in physical education and the arts in both the United States and abroad. The next chapter considers Stebbins' performing and performance practices.

Chapter 9

Genevieve Stebbins on Stage

When the curtain rose on a stage setting of a Grecian interior, the audience saw a graceful figure in a soft, clinging, creamy robe of Greek design, a single tall white lily caught in the girdle that vaguely outlined the waist, the dark brown hair gathered in loose curls into a knot at the back of the head, and sandals on the feet. (Wilbor 1894)

The song of Miriam, with pantomimic action, and the triumphant dance of victory before the Lord, accompanied with the clashing music of the Queen of Sheba, are most impressive. It is a vision of expression that we shall never forget. (unidentified critic quoted in N. A. 1893: 445)

To the traditional elocutionary fare of recited stories, poems, and dramatic selections, American Delsarteans added statue posing, *tableaux*, drills, pantomines, and, to a lesser degree, dances and dance dramas.[1] What distinguished these genres was that they communicated by means of bodily expression rather than spoken words. Preparation for such performance included purely physical exercises such as those described in the previous chapter as well as training in the Delsartean vocabulary, the detailed formulas for expressing character, state of mind, and emotion.

One of the most admired and influential performers of the American Delsartean nonverbal performance forms was Genevieve Stebbins. While she never totally abandoned recitations and dramatic readings, her own

performances (dating from the 1880s to at least 1903) and the commencement exercises of her New York School of Expression featured nonverbal
work including dance. Stebbins herself performed statue poses, dances,
and what she called pantomines (original dance dramas), and she presented her students in poses, dances, and drills. We will first consider
Stebbins' performance and teaching of statue posing, and then her drills,
and finally her dances and pantomines.

STATUE POSING

Statue posing was a staple in Stebbins' recitals as well as in those of
other American Delsarteans, and belongs to a long tradition of "living
pictures" in performance contexts. In this genre, performers singly or in
groups either copy the bodily positions and spatial arrangements depicted in existing art works or create original scenes on various themes.
One or another type of such representational posing can be traced back
as far as antiquity, and the practice was prevalent in Europe on the stage
and in private entertainments from at least the eighteenth century.
In nineteenth- and early-twentieth-century America, it was featured in
popular theatre productions across the country (Holmström 1967;
McCullough 1983). The Delsarteans presented various kinds of poses:
those based on classical Greek and Roman models; "attitudes" developed from the Delsartean expressive vocabulary; and forms variously
identified as *poses plastiques, tableaux vivants,* and *tableaux mouvants* (see
Ruyter 1996a: 73).

One wonders what prompted a professional actress such as Stebbins
to take up this practice, which enjoyed little respect as a serious art form.
While there is mention that, as a child in San Francisco, she had imitated
statues for family gatherings, there is no indication that posing played
any part in her subsequent training as an actress, her instruction from
Mackaye, or her professional stage work. But take it up she did, and by
the 1890s her theoretical basis, rationale, and methodology for it were
fully developed and being presented in lectures and publications and
illustrated in performances.

Stebbins' reverence for classical Greek art, which was the basis of her
interest in statue posing, has been discussed in Chapter 7. Her conviction
that Delsarte's study of "antique statuary" was fundamental to the development of his system and that his laws of expression were essentially
the same as those known in the ancient world also fed her interest in
this form and provided her with the means to develop it (1902: 370–71,
445–46).

Stebbins distinguished her own work from other contemporary posing
on the basis of two characteristics: a focus on general rather than particular qualities in the choice of subjects to be depicted and the use of

designed, motional transitions between poses. While she did not deni-
grate the rendition of individual characters or momentary thoughts or
emotions as a legitimate aspect of expression, she considered the repre-
sentation of "universal truth" to be a loftier goal. In what she termed
"artistic statue-posing," she wished to convey "the idea of absolute calm
and repose of an immortal soul, possessing infinite capacity for expression, but at the same time giving no definite expression except that of
capacity and power in reserve" (1902: 444). Such expression, she believed, was profound and possessed an almost mystical agency. Because
of what she perceived as "purity of soul and nobility of spirit" in the
Greek statues (1902: 453), Stebbins argued that her artistic statue posing
had a "spiritual value in education, since it gives rise to noble ideas"
(1902: 456). The activity of statue posing was thus generalized far beyond
a limited performance genre: it was conceived as an instrument by which
people—and in practice these were women—could reap spiritual as well
as physical benefits.

Genevieve Stebbins presented statue poses not as separated scenes (as
was common in much of posing throughout its history), but in a series
of images in which the transitions figured at least as prominently as the
poses themselves. Whether or not she invented this format, it was her
hallmark. An 1893 reviewer, distinguishing her performance from "or-
dinary" statue posing, wrote that in her poses

> there is no spasmodic transformation of the body.... [The
> poses] flow gracefully onward from the simple to the com-
> plex. They are a natural evolution of beauty produced by the
> changing curve of the spiral line from head to toe, commenc-
> ing with a simple attitude, and continuing with a slow, rhyth-
> mic motion of every portion of the body, until it stands before
> you as the most perfect representation of art. (N. A. 1893: 444)

The same review quotes a *New York Sun* description of Stebbins' "posing
after the manner of twelve classical statues":

> She walked serenely in from a side entrance clad from throat
> to toe in a white Greek robe; her arms were bare and there
> were no signs of white powder or other makeup [a common
> feature of "ordinary" statue posing]. She stood in front of the
> stage, and while the piano was played by somebody out of
> sight slowly assumed the form of Venus Genitrix. A moment
> later she swayed gently about and became the Satyr playing
> the Lute. The lovely audience applauded rapturously, whereat
> Mrs. Stebbins undulated gracefully into the statue of Melpom-
> ene. (N. A. 1893: 445)

The reviewer remarks, "[I]t is impossible to tell where one line ends or the next one begins." From these passages we gain an image of Stebbins' quality of movement in her statue posing: a sustained flow punctuated by brief moments of stillness in a position.

Stebbins' instructions to the student statue poser give the most complete picture of the qualities she sought and considered important in her own and others' performances. After a general suggestion to use real statues or photographs (rather than drawings) for models, and to "study the poise and attitudes of these statues," she embarks on a lengthy discussion that focuses on the transitions—the movement into a pose and between poses—rather than on the poses themselves.

> Stand in front of a large mirror and attempt to make yourself a living duplicate of the picture. . . . (a) There must be simultaneous movement of all parts of body, from head to toe; (b) the motion must be magnetic, i.e., slow, rhythmic, and as unaffected as the subtle evolution of a serpent; (c) every movement must be made in conformity with the principles of evolution, i.e., the movements must unfold from within to without as naturally as the growth and expansion of a flower; (d) there must be no sudden seeking for opposition, no spasmodic attempt for sequence. . . . Every gradation of motion, from normal position to perfect image, must be one beautiful flow of physical transformation.
>
> . . . wherever a series of statues is gone through, one form must gradually melt into the other by the following rules: (a) Regarding each statue as an attitude expressing an impression, the rules of transition of attitude and gesture should be carefully observed, such as the arm moving in an opposite direction to the pointing of the hand; (b) harmonious balancing of arm to arm; (c) preparatory movement in opposite direction to intended attitude; (d) and, finally, rhythm of movement in harmony with character of statue or emotion depicted. (1902: 459–60)

The emphasis is on a continuous design in space rather than any dynamics of time or energy. The poses interrupted the continuity of the transition and stopped action for a few seconds. Then, almost imperceptibly, the next transition would begin. The goal seems to have been a flowing dancelike quality—aurally punctuated by the audience's applause for each pose.

For teaching this popular American Delsartean genre, Stebbins recommended "the esthetic gymnastics based on the system of Delsarte," and stressed as particularly important the Delsartean principles of "harmonic poise" and the Laws of Sequence (or Succession) and Opposition

(1902: 457). As we have seen, in Stebbins' view, physical poise in the Greek statues or in nineteenth-century embodiments of them corresponded to an ideal of "moral poise" (1902: 92–94). By putting one's body into the position of a statue, one would take on the qualities it possessed and profit on both the spiritual and the physical level. While Stebbins recommended that the student use visual verification (looking in a mirror) to work on her performance rather than any internal sense of her body in relation to the visual data, she writes that "artistic statue-posing is not mere external imitation of a Greek marble. It is something infinitely greater. It is a creative work of intellectual love. It is a spiritual aspiration toward a superior and definite type of beauty, in which lives and moves a human soul" (1902: 461). Therefore, in practicing statue posing, the students trained their characters as well as their bodies. The ability to master successional movement provided a flow that was comparable to music (1902: 457) and that melded the series of poses into a unified composition in time and space.

The photographs of 32 classical statues included in the 1902 edition of *Delsarte System of Expression* illustrate the sort of images Stebbins chose for teaching and performance (see Ruyter 1996a: 79). They include an almost equal number of male and female figures in various states of dress or undress. Most are gods and goddesses, but there are also some historical and mythological characters.

Most of the figures are in tranquil poses—with the weight predominantly resting on one leg (the foundation of "harmonic poise") and one or both arms in some kind of gesture. Ten of the figures represent actions (four play musical instruments, one shoots a bow, three engage in violent combat, one runs, and one is throwing a discus), but of these 10, only eight really suggest movement through time and space—a moment in an action that began before the position we see and is moving through it on to further action.

The program information available shows that Stebbins would go through 10 to 20 statues when she performed a series of poses, and these included the same range of material that is illustrated in *Delsarte System of Expression*. For statue posing, Stebbins wore the generalized long sleeveless "Greek" gown described at the beginning of this chapter and shown in Illustration 4. This was appropriate considering that she was presenting a series of different poses without leaving the stage and that her concern was to depict universal qualities rather than individual characters.

There are many unclear aspects regarding Stebbins' statue posing. She gives no guidance on how to emulate the statues themselves or if any particular physical quality should be attempted on the basis of a model's gender, character, emotion, or action. Nor does she provide suggestions on matters such as the timing of poses and transitions, breathing, use of props, and choice of or relationship with music. From what she and others have written, Stebbins' concern was to copy the position in space of the model statue without any attempt to act or dress the part. It was not a role, as an actor might play, but rather a sculptural design that embodied the universal principles to which she was drawn. Other Delsartean statue posers, however, were not always so austere in their renditions as can be seen from illustrations in Werner's magazines and elsewhere. Often they show facial and bodily expression that indicate character, emotion, and momentary frame of mind.

DRILLS

"Drills" were also frequently presented in performances by Stebbins and other Delsarteans. These took a variety of forms: some were simply sequences of connected statue poses; some involved marching and formations of children or women dressed as characters; some featured pantomime; and others even consisted of or included dance.

In the 1890s Stebbins developed a number of drills for her students to perform. Four of these were published in 1894 as an appendix to her *Society Gymnastics* of 1893. These and five others appeared in *The Genevieve Stebbins System of Physical Training* (all references here are to the 1913 edition of that work). Most of Stebbins' drills are described for one person, but she cautions that it "would be a dangerous experiment for the average individual without study" to perform the drills in public—that "they require a well-developed physique, natural grace, and perfect aesthetic training to reveal that beauty of motion which has given them public favor." She adds, however, that group performance of the drills in strict unison hides individual flaws and is particularly effective as a presentation at commencement exercises (1913a: 82).

The nine published drills include four that consist of poses with transitions between; four that feature decorative, and sometimes dancelike expressive or abstract, movement; and one dance. Of the first group, two are based on classical statues in battle or athletic poses. "The Roman Drill—The Amazon" (1913a: 110–14) presents images of a warrior woman in actions such as holding a spear, running, drawing a bow, charging, and retreating, while the theme of "The Athenian Drill—The Victory" (1913a: 119–23) is "domination and power," which is realized through similar images. The latter drill also features a pose of the *Winged Victory* and is framed with a march on and off stage. It is quite remarkable that Stebbins along with other Delsarteans seemed drawn to male or female statues depicting scenes related to battle. Male warriors as well as the fierce female Amazons were popular subjects perhaps because of the dynamism of their poses—or did they represent a sense of power unavailable to these women that could be embodied and enjoyed in the safety of the Delsartean circle?

The "Energizing Dramatic Drill" (1913a: 97–102) also features a series of poses in the context of battle. Rather than being based on statues, however, it employs Delsartean attitudes in five series to portray a dramatic narrative that includes flight, attack, retreat, and defeat. The poses feature clenched fists and the expressions of fright, anger, repulsion, horror, and despair. Again, one must question the fascination with violence. The "Eastern Temple Drill" (1913a; 84–90) has a completely different quality. Its theme is religious aspiration and it incorporates movements and symbols Stebbins derived from "the ceremonials found variously among the Mohammedans, the Druses, the Marabouts and the Dervishes." The poses include the "prayer form" (palms together with fingers pointing upward), the "Flame Attitude" (erect body with hands in prayer but above the head), the "cross form" (body erect with arms stretched to the side), and the "Prostrate Attitude" (cross form with one leg behind and torso and head leaning back). Stebbins stresses the spiritual values of this drill, but also mentions the practical: it helps develop the chest and back.

The remaining five drills embody much lighter content and dance movement. "The English Drill—The May" (1913a; 91–96) refers to an old English May Day festival. Framed by an entrance and exit of "fancy march step[s] with waving arms," the choreography includes curtseys, arm and body motions, and pointing steps. Stebbins advises that the drill should embody the "merrymaking of England" and the "joy of springtime"; that it should be accompanied by "old English songs" or "light marches"; and that the costume should resemble that of a "Dresden China Shepherdess."

"The Spanish Drill—The Carmen" (1913a; 103–109) features manipulations of a Spanish mantilla (a long lace scarf attached to the head over a decorative comb), combined with curtseys, kneeling, arm and body motions, pointing steps, and heel and toe step patterns. The composition is in four figures, and Stebbins suggests "a pretty interlude" that can be given after each figure. It consists of: "(a) Grand Chain. (b) Heel and toe side-step. (c) Opposite lines cross, fanning gracefully and looking over the shoulders. (d) Courtesy to partners and walk gracefully out, holding partner's hand high and fanning." It is interesting that partners, specific group formations, and fans are not mentioned in any of the four figures that make up the core of the drill. Stebbins suggests, in addition to the lace mantilla, yellow costumes trimmed with black lace and high comb and rose for the hair, but she gives no indication of what kind of music to use. The image of "Carmen" must have come from the Bizet opera, but is here presented in a completely sanitized version, as an innocent representative of a nontransgressive exotic figure. Stebbins exhorts her students that when performing this drill, "an enjoyment of all that is graceful and lovely should pervade your thought."

"The Greek Drill—The Nymphs" (1913a; 124–30), while based on classical imagery, involves far more movement than poses. In Stebbins' words, "it is a study of the beautiful motion often carved to represent the various actions and sportive grace of those ideal creations of the Greek fancy, supposed to people wood, water, air, and fire." The composition includes an entrance and exit in waltz time and six figures that variously combine movements such as swaying, circling of the arms and torso, serpentine arm motions, a swimming motion, pivoting on the toes, kneeling, and bowing. The costume is specified as "Greek with drapery hanging from the shoulders."

The "Aesthetic Drill" (1913a; 131–32), the only abstract piece in the collection, consists of four groups of arm movements: "Flying Series," "Half-Serpentine Series," "Serpentine Arm Series," and "Spiral Series." Its character is that of an exercise routine to develop skill in these favored Delsartean arm motions, or to demonstrate them, rather than an expressive performance piece.

The one dance in the collection, "Minuet Fan-Drill" (1913a; 115–18), is a loose adaptation of the minuet for any number of couples (presumably all girls). In a choreographic spatial pattern involving locomotion as well as movement in fixed positions, the dance includes an entrance step, marching in formations, a toe-pointing pattern, a series of torso circles and bends from a kneeling position, and elaborate movements of the fan. It involves the entire body in movements that require balance, flexibility, and stamina. Unfortunately, there is no indication of what music was used, the counts for the movements, or their dynamic quality.

These drills provide the only idea of Stebbins' approach to movement composition, and they are frustratingly vague and inconsistent. She points out in her introduction to them that they are not full descriptions, but are only notes to pupils who are already familiar with her terminology and manner of teaching (1913a: 82–83). Sparse as they are, however, they give some insight into her movement vocabulary and compositional style. In the first place, there is an overwhelming emphasis on movements of the arms and torso, not surprising given the fact that this vocabulary derived in large part from the Delsarte-Mackaye gestural canon. In that canon, the upper body represents the "higher" aspects of the human being: the soul and mind, the moral and mental functions, the spiritual and intellectual qualities. Another reason for featuring the upper body was that, for these proper ladies, the legs were not privileged as a body part. Quite the contrary, they were hidden and not to be mentioned by name in polite society. While, in her later works, Stebbins included more exercises that involved the legs, there was no developed strength-producing regimen (such as that found in ballet or modern dance training) in the Delsarte work. The clothing worn by the Delsartean practitioners also did not allow for much variety of leg work. The gowns descended all the way to the floor, limiting both the mobility and visibility of the legs. Despite the lack of emphasis on the legs as expressive agents, however, Delsartean performers did walk in various ways, lunge, kneel, and perform a few small foot patterns with their heels and toes. The lunges and kneeling found in Stebbins' drills required a certain degree of strength and balance. For example, in Figure V of "The Greek Drill—The Nymphs," the following movements are described:

1. Slowly kneel by bending the right knee and slipping the left foot farther and farther behind you, swaying the arms laterally while doing so. . . .
2. Gradually rise during eight measures, finger-tips touching and trunk circling. A slight separation of hands takes place when half way up and the arms perform spiral serpentine motions and are finally held up in flame prayer form, finger-tips touching. Eight measures should be spent in rising and arm motion and attitude. Perform this twice on each side. (1913a: 127–28)

In the "Minuet Fan-Drill," the performers

> kneel and sweep fans, held in both hands, up and down in opposition to the bending body; for instance, the body on both knees, bracing toes against the floor, sways back as far as it can, while the arms swing forward, and vice versa. Repeat three times. . . . Fan in both hands held over head, body sways from side to side twice. (1913a: 118)

Following that, the position is changed to one knee only, and the torso sways, circles, and twists with the arms and head counterbalancing (1913a: 118). One wonders about these movements, surely no knee pads were available. Furthermore, how did the ladies manage to stand up gracefully with presumably somewhat weak thighs *and* a volume of skirt tangling around their feet and legs.

The choreography of these drills is very simple. The spatial orientation is generally toward the audience with the position of the performer fixed in space. There is some locomotor movement, as noted above, as well as moving into or out of simple formations such as a circle or opposing lines. Five of the drills call for entrances and exits—sometimes with a specific step and/or musical tempo such as waltz or marching time, and two, the Spanish Drill and the minuet, have some locomotion within the piece itself. Some of the drills just begin, and there is no indication if these were framed by the opening and closing of a curtain, by blackouts, or by some kind of entrance and exit. There is symmetrical repetition in all of the drills; that is, movement is done to the right and then repeated to the left. The simplicity of the choreography may have been due to the fact that these were exercises designed for students, but from the sparse information about Stebbins' own performance, it seems that she herself did not use different or more varied elements than are demonstrated in the drills.

DANCES AND PANTOMIMES

While Genevieve Stebbins would never have characterized herself as a dancer, she moved ever closer to dance during the 1880s and by 1890 was performing dances during her Delsartean matinees. Her statue posing and drills were certainly dancelike; they were movement organized in time, space, and energy and designed for an artistic end.

However, Stebbins did not stop with flowing statue posing and choreographed "drills." At least as early as the Stebbins-Thompson Delsarte matinee of 25 March 1890 (at the Madison Square Theatre), she presented actual dances identified as such. On this program, in addition to statue poses and a pantomime, "Ode to the Passions," Stebbins gave a talk on Delsartean gymnastics, illustrating her points with a minuet, a Spanish dance, and a Greek dance (*Werner's Voice Magazine* 12 [June 1890]: 163).

In subsequent performances, Stebbins added dances from the ancient Middle East as well. A *Boston Globe* critic in 1893 described one of Stebbins' presentations of "the history of dramatic expression . . . illustrated by poses and dances of the various periods" as follows:

> Mrs. Stebbins gave first the pose and movements of the Egyptian priestesses who swung the censers slowly and rhythmically in their temple worship. She then gave the Greek idea of dancing and artistic management of the body, derived from [illustrations on Greek friezes, pottery, and statues]. Her Greek dance was enchanting almost to voluptuousness. Then followed the sprightly Spanish and gypsy dances of a later day in which there was as much movement of the arms and body as of the lower limbs. Mrs. Stebbins closed . . . with the stately bows and slow paces of the minuet. (quoted in N. A. 1893: 445)

The "dances" described here sound similar to the drills discussed above. Perhaps they were the same, and she simply called them "dances" in her own performances and "drills" for students.

In a July 1894 performance at Chautauqua, Stebbins' context for presenting dance was neither Delsartean gymnastics nor the history of dramatic expression, but rather the history of dance itself. As described in a news item, Stebbins gave "an exhibition of the evolution of dancing, showing its place in physical culture," that included "an old English country dance, a gypsy dance, the Scotch Highlander's dance, an Alpine rustic dance, a French and a Spanish minuet" (*Werner's Magazine* 16 [September 1894]: 334). Presumably such renditions were meant to represent actual folk or social dances.

There is no clue as to the sources of the dances Stebbins performed. It seems most likely that she created them herself on the basis of research, the same kind of research engaged in later by Ruth St. Denis and Isadora Duncan when they wished to extend beyond what was easily accessible in the theatrical dance of their own time and place. She clearly based the classical Greek dance on illustrations from Greek art and what she had read about dance in classical Greek times. The others probably originated in a similar way—except, perhaps the minuet, for which step patterns were probably available. As we have seen, Stebbins includes various references to dance in other cultures in her writings.

Also in the 1890s, Stebbins developed a repertoire of dance-dramas that she called pantomimes. These were described as "musical, dramatic and pantomimic monologues," each with three or four acts, full costuming, and music played by three to six instrumentalists. The series included the following works: "Miriam, the Prophetess," "Jeptha's Daughter," "Esther at Shushan," "The Myth of Isis," "Ariadne," "Psyche," "Ceres," "Brunhilda," and "The Descent of Ishtar" (N. A. 1893: 444). Thus she chose themes from antiquity (classical and Egyptian), the Bible, and mythology, each centered on a strong female character.

There is a detailed review of Stebbins' performance of "Miriam, the Prophetess" on 25 January 1894, at the Berkeley Lyceum in New York City (Wilbor 1894). The piece was organized in five scenes: (1) Miriam awakening from the sleep during which Jehovah had spoken with her; (2) the consecration of Miriam; (3) Miriam's delivery of Jehovah's message to Pharaoh (to free the Israelites), his refusal, and her curse upon him and his people; (4) Miriam's grief over the plagues that resulted from the curse; and (5) the triumph of the Israelites and the downfall of the Egyptians. While several characters were implied in the story, there was only one performer—Stebbins, who used pantomime, dance, and words to create the total effect. The critic writes that this "experiment was unique, almost daring, and the audience, having nothing with which to compare it . . . seemed hardly able to decide whether applause or censure was more appropriate. . . . Yet there was nothing there that could offend the most prudish or shock the most delicate conscience" (Wilbor 1894).

The description of Stebbins' performance in this work (one of the few we have of her dancing) gives an idea of her range as a dance artist. The reviewer writes that in the scene of consecration, after pantomiming the "mystic rights [sic] of temple worship . . . Miriam gives a strange, slow dance many times around the altar sometimes with wreaths and sometimes empty-handed" (Wilbor 1894). In the next scene, she enters with a scroll that bears Jehovah's message to Pharaoh:

> The dance accompanying this scene is a marvel of grace and beauty. The music pulses more strongly than before, and Miriam, swinging her censer now to the altar, now over the scroll, now around her head, bends and sways and bends again in a very ecstacy of religious fervor. A more emotional and yet chaste dance would be difficult to imagine. In the midst of the dance she sees Pharaoh, and dropping upon her knees, beseeches him to free her people. (Wilbor 1894)

The closing scene also featured dance, Miriam's dance of celebration by the Red Sea. In the critic's words, "Her dance with the cymbals is one of the utmost abandon of joy. Then falling to her knees, she chants a portion of the fifteenth chapter of Exodus, after which she resumes her dance, and the curtain falls for the last time" (Wilbor 1894). One marvels at the very stamina, let alone artistry, necessary to carry a whole production such as this, which involved Stebbins alone in each scene and required the breath and ability to move from dance to speech to chant in one seamless performance. These works suggest that there was a continuing development in Stebbins' conceptualization and realization of dance expression, and also demonstrate that she must have had a certain level of technical proficiency and a high degree of expressive artistry that enabled her to perform such material effectively.

It finally remains to look at one piece that Stebbins presented that was pure dance expression, not an illustration of lecture material nor one element in a mixed genre production. This is the "Dance of Day," which so strongly impressed the young Ruth St. Denis at a performance given 25 November 1892 at the Madison Square Theatre. In her autobiography, St. Denis describes Stebbins' statue poses as well as the dance:

> The curtain rose on a dark greenish background . . . and there stood an exquisite woman in a costume made of soft ivory-white material that fell in gracious lines to her feet, her figure beautifully proportioned, her blond head proud and shapely. The strong light pouring upon her made her gleam like a pearl against the dark setting.
>   She moved in a series of plastiques which were based upon her understanding of the laws of motion discovered by Delsarte. Her poses were derived from Greek statuary and en-

compassed everything from the tragedy of Niobe to the joyousness of Terpsichore. Later she did a dance called the *Dance of Day*. At the opening of the scene, she was lying on the floor asleep, and then, awakened by the morning sun, she rose with a lovely childlike movement to her knees and bathed herself in its rays. A light rhythmic step signified the morning and the noontide; and then began the slower movements of the afternoon, presently mingled with sadness as the late rays brought her slowly to her knees and again into her reclining posture of sleep. (St. Denis 16–17)

With this work, Stebbins entered fully into the kind of exploration that would characterize the modern dance movement yet to come.

Stebbins' unique approach to statue posing and drills, her dancing as a feature of full-length pantomimes, her rendition of historical dance and the dance of other cultures, and her presentation of dance as an independent art form—all demonstrate an impressive resourcefulness and creativity in the art of expressive movement. In her ideals, in her approach to movement as an expressive medium, and in her performances, Stebbins introduced much of what would be credited by future generations to the invention of Isadora Duncan and Ruth St. Denis. It was Stebbins who was the first pioneer in the tradition that is called "modern dance." The lack of recognition of her contribution is undoubtedly because she was mainly an educator rather than a performing artist; she worked in a narrower circle than the internationally renowned Duncan and St. Denis; and dance historians have tended to focus on great and famous artists rather than on figures who might have been important as part of the matrix of major developments.

NOTE

1. Much of the material in this chapter, some worded somewhat differently, was first published in Susan Leigh Foster, ed., *Corporealities* (London: Routledge, 1996), under the title "Antique Longings: Genevieve Stebbins and American Delsartean Performance."

who has most directly addressed the issue of the two faces of Delsartism. In discussing what has often been seen as the "trivialization of American Delsarte's high artistic aims," she argues for attention to all aspects of the Delsarte phenomenon:

> [T]he many and varied manifestations of Delsarte in America—the ways in which it was used and abused, recycled and reconstructed—are valuable evidence of the complex cultural values of the time, especially in regard to class and gender. In the many manifestations, "authentic" and "inauthentic," of American Delsarte, practitioners enacted a variety of conflicting, and conflicted, aspirations for social- and self-improvement. (1996: 204)

I agree with this wholeheartedly, and would add that, in addition to being relevant to broad cultural studies, attention to the spectrum of American Delsartism also provides insights into specific areas of the culture, including the arts, physical education, fashions, the use of leisure time, and perceptions of the mind-body relationship.

My interest in American Delsartism began from the point of view of a dance historian, but the perspective has broadened to include also a curiosity about people's use of their bodies in their everyday lives: how individuals hold themselves, present themselves to the world, and move in space and time—and what this all has to do with their culture in general and how they operate in the world. From that perspective I have many (unanswerable) questions in regard to American Delsartean practice. To what extent, for example, did it actually work to improve a student's carriage, grace, poise, fitness, expressive effectiveness? To what extent did it give practitioners a greater awareness of the totality of their bodies than they would have had without it? To what extent did it foster a sense of mind-body unity in the student? Did it provide enjoyable, sensually pleasant, profound experiences? What was the relationship between the rhetoric and the physical practice, and did the former actually contribute to the latter? Did the Delsartean practice effect in any way how a girl or woman confronted her world and lived her life?

While we cannot really answer such questions, an experience of the exercises and practices themselves can at least give some idea of their potential, and allow us to imagine how someone of another time, place, class, and culture might have experienced them (while acknowledging that we can never really know). I gave a conference workshop a few years ago on Stebbins' statue posing. We began with her exercises for relaxation, poise, oppositions, and successions, then learned the poses of four statue models (shown in slides), and finally developed moving transitions between the poses, following as far as possible Stebbins' published instructions. The result was remarkable both to see and do. Of course, it had to be far from what a nineteenth-century Delsartean would have experienced, but I believe the exercise gave us some insight into Delsartean practice that we would not have had otherwise. What it particularly did for me was to show me that this was not merely a silly surface activity; it engaged mind, body, and feelings.

This work has included some quite detailed descriptions of Delsarte's, Mackaye's, and Stebbins' theory and practice, and I think it is important to understand how the physical action as well as the purposes associated with Delsartism changed and evolved over time. In my opinion, the physical training developed out of a remarkably profound analysis of movement that began with Delsarte and continued through Stebbins and then went on to enter the streams of physical culture and dance in both America and Europe. I do not consider the Delsartean exercises banal and unimportant. Rather, they represented (as they developed) stages— in the understanding of how the body works and the relation of that to health; in the analysis of bodily design in space and time; in the development of movement as an expressive medium; and in finding effective physical training methods for the general public as well as for performing artists. I have "tried on" exercises from the various phases—from Mackaye to Stebbins' latest material—and find that as the work developed the exercise material required (created) greater and greater bodily involvement and sensation. I think it is important when dealing with a physical discipline such as the Delsarte work to consider it from the bodily experiential side as well as from its "inscripted" traces.

This study has not addressed many questions regarding the American Delsarte phenomenon. One is the relationship of the Delsartean exercise material with that of other systems of the mid- and late nineteenth century—particularly the physical training of Dio Lewis and the training in expression developed by Oskar Guttman (who considered the Delsarte system to be in competition with his own). Another would be how the Delsartean exercise material compares with later practices in dance and actor training. Still others would include the relationship of the Delsarte "craze" to the various facets of women's culture of the late nineteenth century. I hope this basically factual study will stimulate others to pursue some of those issues. I, for one, cannot wait to embark on further Delsartean journeys.

Bibliography

ABBREVIATIONS

DCL	Dartmouth College Library
ESW	Edgar S. Werner
JOHPER	*Journal of Health, Physical Education and Recreation*
LC	Library of Congress
LSU-BR	Louisiana State University, Baton Rouge
NYPL-PAC	New York Public Library, Performing Arts Collections
U	University
Voice	*The Voice*
WM	*Werner's Magazine*
WVM	*Werner's Voice Magazine*

ARCHIVAL COLLECTIONS

Delsarte Collection, Louisiana State University, Baton Rouge, Louisiana
Richard Hovey Collection, Dartmouth College, Hanover, New Hampshire
Mackaye Archive, Dartmouth College, Hanover, New Hampshire
Ted Shawn Collection, New York Public Library for the Performing Arts, Dance
    Collection

PERIODICALS

Action and Utterance. Organ of the New York School of Expression, 1901–1903.
The Elocutionist. London, 1882–1891.

Expression. Boston, 1895–1897. Organ of the Currys' School of Expression.
Werner's series of magazines, all published in New York: *The Voice*, 1879–1888;
  Werner's Voice Magazine, 1889–1892; *Werner's Magazine*, 1893–1902.

REFERENCES CITED AND RELATED MATERIALS

Adams, Florence A. Fowle. (1891). *Gesture and Pantomimic Action*. New York:
  ESW.
Adams, Fred Winslow. (1892a). "Delsarte and Shakespeare." Part IV of "Delsart-
  ism in America." *WVM* 14 (March): 63–64.
———. (1892b). "Mme. Géraldy in America." *WVM* 14 (May): 137.
———. (1893a). "The Stage View of Delsarte." *WM* 15 (February): 41–43.
———. (1893b). "William Rounseville Alger." *WM* 15 (March): 86–89.
———. (1894). "Truth about Delsarte" (interview with Henrietta Hovey). *Boston
  Courier* (February 18).
Ainsworth, Dorothy S. (1930). *The History of Physical Education in Colleges for
  Women*. New York: A. S. Barnes.
Alberti, Eva Allen. (1894). *Madame Alberti's Delsarte School of Expression*. New
  York: ESW (In LC).
Alexander, F. Matthias. (1969). *The Resurrection of the Body: Writings of F. Matthias
  Alexander*. Edited by Edward Maisel. New York: University Books.
Alger, William Rounseville. (1877). *Life of Edwin Forrest, the American Tragedian*.
  Philadelphia: Lippincott; New York: Benjamin Blom, 1972. Pp. 657–62, in
  1877 edition on Delsarte.
———. (1881). "The Delsarte Philosophy" (interviews with Alger and Hovey
  [Mrs. Henrietta Crane]). *Voice* 3 (December): 176–78.
———. (1884). "William R. Alger. Why Should an Author so Profound and Brilliant Hesitate to Publish an Exposition of the Delsarte Philosophy? DEL-
  SARTEANS PROTEST AGAINST FURTHER DELAY. Extracts from His
  Writings to Prove Him Fully Competent for Such an Undertaking" (excerpts from Alger's *Life of Edwin Forrest*). *Voice* 6 (June): 81–83.
———. (1885). "A True System of Gymnastics." *Voice* 7 (April): 55–56.
———. (1893a) "Place and Power of Personality in Expression." *WM* 15 (July):
  229–33.
———. (1893b). "Delsartism in America." *WM* 15 (October): 341–43.
———. (1894). "The Aesthetic Gymnastics of Delsarte." *WM* (January): 3–4.
Ambegaokar, Saga Mirjam. (1985). "Maggie Gripenberg: A Finnish Pioneer in
  Modern Dance." Master's thesis, Dance History, U. of California, River-
  side.
Anderson, William Gilbert. (1893). *Light Gymnastics. A Guide to Systematic Instruction in Physical Training. For Use in Schools, Gymnasia, etc.* New York: Ef-
  fingham Maynard.
———. (1897). *Anderson's Physical Education. Health and Strength. Grace and Symmetry*. New York: A. D. Dana.
Arnaud, Angélique. (1882). *François Del Sarte; Ses découvertes en esthétique, sa science, sa méthode. Paris: Librairie Ch. Delagrave.
———. (1883). "The Delsarte System." In *Delsarte System of Oratory*. 2nd and sub-

sequent editions. Translated and edited by Abby L. Alger from Arnaud 1882.

———. (1893). "The Delsarte System." In *Delsarte System of Oratory*, 4th ed. All references are to this edition.

Aslan, Odette. (1974). *L'acteur au XXᵉ siècle: Évolution de la technique; Problème d'éthique*. Paris: Éditions Seghers.

Austin, G. L. (1882). *A Doctor's Talk with Maiden, Wife, and Mother*. Boston: Lothrop, Lee & Shepard.

Baker, Michael. (1978). *The Rise of the Victorian Actor*. London: Croom Helm.

Balliet, Mrs. L. Dow. (1901). "The Body Beautiful According to the Delsartian Philosophy." *WM* 27, no. 4 (June): 227–43.

Bancroft, Jessie H. (1896). *School Gymnastics. Free Hand. A System of Physical Exercises for Schools*. New York: E. L. Kellogg.

Banner, Lois W. (1983). *American Beauty*. New York: Knopf.

Banta, Martha. (1987). *Imaging American Women; Ideas and Ideals in Cultural History*. New York: Columbia U. Press.

Baril, Jacques. (1984). *La danse moderne d'Isadora Duncan à Twyla Tharp*. Paris: Éditions Vigot. (1977).

Bishop, Emily M. (1892a). *Americanized Delsarte Culture*. Meadville, PA: Chautauqua-Century Press.

———. (1892b). "Delsarte Culture—Shall It Be Restricted or Expanded?" Part III of "Delsartism in America." *WVM* 14 (March): 61–63.

———. (1899). "How Gestures Are Regarded." *WM* 23, no. 4 (June): 339–42.

———. (1900). "Psychological Training of the Body." *WM* 25, no. 2 (April): 142–45.

Blair, Karen J. (1980). *The Clubwoman as Feminist; True Womanhood Redefined, 1868–1914*. New York: Holmes & Meier.

Bode, Rudolf. (1931). *Expression-Gymnastics*. Translated from the German by S. Forthal and E. Waterman. New York: A. S. Barnes.

Böhme, Fritz. (1926). *Der Tanz der Zukunft*. Munich: Delphin.

Bradshaw, William R. (1891). "An Interview with Mrs. Edmund Russell." *The Decorator and Furnisher* 19 (April): 181–83.

Brandenburg, Hans. (1913). *Der Moderne Tanz*. Munich: Georg Müller.

Brown, Margaret C., and Josephine Beiderhase. (1960). "William G. Anderson." *JOHPER* 31 (April): 34, 126.

Brown, Margaret C., and Betty K. Sommer. (1969). *Movement Education: Its Evolution and a Modern Approach*. Reading, MA: Addison-Wesley.

Brown, Moses True. (1882a). "The New Philosophy of Expression." *Voice* 4 (May–June): 67–68.

———. (1882b). "Delaumosne and Delsarte." *Voice* 4 (May–June): 74.

———. (1882c). "The Del Sarte Philosophy of Expression." *Voice* 4 (October): 125–27.

———. (1883). "The New School of Elocution. The Philosophy of Human Expression as Formulated by François Delsarte." *Voice* 5 (January): 1–3.

———. (1885). "Delsarte's Nine Laws of Gesture." *Voice* 7 (February): 23.

———. (1886). *The Synthetic Philosophy of Expression as Applied to the Arts of Reading, Oratory, and Personation*. Boston and New York: Houghton Mifflin.

————. (1893). "Is There a Philosophy of Expression?" *WM* 15 (September): 296–300.

Buchanan, Joseph Rodes. (1882a). *Moral Education: Its Laws and Methods*. New York: The Author.

————. (1882b). *The New Education: Moral, Industrial, Hygienic, Intellectual*. 3rd ed. Boston: The Author.

————. (1885). *Manual of Psychometry: The Dawn of a New Civilization*. 4th ed. Los Angeles: The Author; Boston: Frank H. Hodges, 1893.

————. (1891). *Therapeutic Sarcognomy. The Application of Sarcognomy, the Science of the Soul, Brain and Body, to the Therapeutic Philosophy and Treatment of Bodily and Mental Diseases* . . . 3rd ed. Kansas City: The Author; Boston: J. G. Cupples Co.

Buning, J.W.F. Werumeus. (1926). *Dansen en danseressen*. Amsterdam: Em. Querido's Uitgevers-Maatschappij.

Burgoyne, Thomas H. (1889). *The Light of Egypt, or the Science of the Soul and the Stars*. Vol. 1. San Francisco: The Religio-Philosophical Publishing House; Denver: Astro Philosophical Publishing Co., 1963 (reprint of 5th ed. with additional material); and Denver: H. O. Wagner, 1965 (reprint of 1963 ed.).

————. (1969). *The Light of Egypt or the Science of the Soul and the Stars*. Vol. 2 Portland, OR: Green Dolphin Bookshop. Original edition (1900). Denver: Astro Philosophical Publishing Co.; reprint, Denver: 1963; and Denver: H. O. Wagner, 1965 (reprint with additional material from "Hermetic Teachers").

Burns, Judy. (1989). "Niobe and the Amazons." Master's thesis, New York U.

————. (1992). "Reconstructions." *Women and Performance* 5, no. 2: 112–47.

————. (1996). "The Culture of Nobility/The Nobility of Self-Cultivation." In Gay Morris, ed., *Moving Words; Re-writing Dance*, 203–26. London and New York: Routledge.

Call, Annie Payson. (1891). *Power through Repose*. Boston: Roberts Brothers.

Carman, Bliss. (1908). *The Making of Personality*. Boston: The Page Company. (1906). In the Preface Carman acknowledges Mary Perry King as collaborator in this work.

Case, Lizzie York. (1885). "A New School of Art; Delsartean Camping Ground by the Sea." *Voice* 7 (January): 13.

Charles, Frank T. (1892). "Foreign Correspondence: Delsarte." *WVM* 14 (October): 308–10.

Christoffersen, Erik Exe. (1993). *The Actor's Way*. London: Routledge.

The Church of Light. (1995). "The Brotherhood of Light. The Church of Light: Its History and Principles." Brochure. Revised July 1995 by vlb.

Colby, Gertrude Kline. (1922). *Natural Rhythms and Dances*. New York: A. S. Barnes.

————. (1930). *The Conflict: A Health Masque in Pantomime*. New York: A. S. Barnes.

Connerton, Paul. (1989). *How Societies Remember*. Cambridge: Cambridge U. Press.

Coyrière, E. Miriam. (1892). "Mme Géraldy's Visit to America." *WVM* 14 (April): 103.

Crane, Henrietta. *See* Hovey, Henrietta.

Curry, Samuel S. (1885). "Delsarte and Mackaye." *Voice* 7 (March): 42–44.

———. (1891). *The Province of Expression; A Search for Principles Underlying Adequate Methods of Developing Dramatic and Oratoric Delivery.* Boston: School of Expression.

———. (1896). "Professor Lewis Baxter Monroe, A.M.; Some Characteristics of His Teaching." *Expression* 2, no. 3 (December): 237–50.

———. (1897). "Elocution and Vocal Training.—The Importance of Studying Their History." *WM* 20, no. 1 (September): 87–94.

Curtiss, Mina. (1958). *Bizet and His World.* New York: Knopf.

Daly, Ann. (1995). *Done into Dance: Isadora Duncan in America.* Bloomington: Indiana U. Press.

Dasgupta, Gautam. (1993). "Commedia Delsarte." *Performing Arts Journal* 45 (September): 95–102.

Daymon, Cedro. (1891). "Delsarte Echoes from Chautauqua; I. Americanizing Delsarte." *WVM* 13 (October): 253.

Delaumosne, Abbé. (1874). *Pratique de L'art Oratoire de Delsarte.* Paris. English trans. by Frances A. Shaw: "The Delsarte System" in *Delsarte System of Oratory*, 1st ed. (New York: ESW, 1882). All references here are to this translation in the 4th edition of 1893.

Delsarte, François. (1833). *Méthode philosophique du chant.* Paris: The Author.

———. (1865). "Esthétique appliquée, les sources de l'art." Address before the *Société philotechnique* in Paris and published in their annals in 1866. English translation in Stebbins, *Delsarte System of Expression*, from the 1887 2nd through the 1902 6th edition. References here are to the 1902 ed.

———. (1887). "The Literary Remains of François Delsarte." Translated by Abby L. Alger in *Delsarte System of Oratory* beginning with this 3rd ed. References here are to the 1893 4th ed.

Delsarte, Madeleine. (n.d.). Unpublished manuscript written after 1872. A copy typed by Madeleine's daughter Geneviève was given to Geneviève's daughter, Mme. Jacqueline Gancel Bouts, the great-granddaughter of François Delsarte. She provided me with a copy. Translations are mine.

"Delsarte Matinee." (1892). *WVM* 14 (May): 149–50.

Delsarte System of Oratory, 4th ed. (1893). New York: ESW. (1st ed. 1882). Includes Delaumosne's book; Delsarte's "Literary Remains"; Arnaud's book; Mme. Géraldy's lecture and lessons in the United States; and articles by Alfred Giraudet, Francis A. Durivage, and Hector Berlioz.

Delsarte-Portzert, Simone. (1986). Unpublished genealogy of the Delsarte family sent to me by Alain Porte.

"Delsarte's Art Universal." (1886). *Voice* 8 (January): 15.

"Delsartiana." (1892a). *WVM* 14 (May): 138–41. Includes articles by Fannie Edgar Thomas and Elsie M. Wilbor.

"Delsartiana." (1892b). *WVM* 14 (June): 159–62. Includes articles by Nettie Hooper, Elsie M. Wilbor, and unidentified authors.

"Delsartism in America." (1892). *WVM* 14 (March): 59–64. Includes articles by E. S. Werner, Mary S. Thompson, Emily M. Bishop, and Fred Winslow Adams.

Dictionary of American Biography. (1928). Auspices of American Council of Learned Societies. Edited by Allen Johnson. 21 vols. Vols. 1–13. New York: Charles Scribner's Sons.

Diehl, Anna Randall. *See* Randall-Diehl, Anna.

Dillport, Rayda Wallace. (1946). "The Pupils of François Delsarte." Master's thesis, LSU-BR, Department of Speech.

Drew, Talma. (1884). "Henrietta Crane: Disciple of Delsarte." *Voice* 6 (April): 61.

Duncan, Isadora. (1927). *My Life*. Garden City, NY: Garden City Publishing Co.

Durivage, Francis A. (1871). "Delsarte." *Atlantic Monthly* (May). Reprinted in *Delsarte System of Oratory*, 574–95; Zorn; and excerpts in *Voice* 3 (November): 152–54.

Ecob, Helen Gilbert. (1893). *The Well-Dressed Woman: A Study in the Practical Application to Dress of the Laws of Health, Art, and Morals*. 2nd ed., rev. & enl. New York: Fowler and Wells. (1892).

"Eleanor Georgen." (1893). *WM* 15 (October): 345–346.

Emerson, Charles Wesley. (1891). *Physical Culture of the Emerson College of Oratory, Boston*. 6th ed. Boston: Emerson College of Oratory.

———. (1894a). "The Emerson Theory of Gesture." *WM* 16 (September): 320–21.

———. (1894b). "The Evolution of Natural Gesture." *WM* 16 (October): 355–56.

———. (1900). *Expressive Physical Culture or Philosophy of Gesture*. Boston: Emerson College of Oratory.

"Equipment of Our Faculty." (1902). *Action and Utterance* 1 (February): 223–24.

Eschbach, Elizabeth S. (1993). *The Higher Education of Women in England and America 1865–1920*. New York: Garland.

"False Delsartism." (1890). *WVM* 12 (January): 23.

Farrah, Ibrahim. (1993). "A Matter of Study to Fill a Hundred Years." *Arabesque* 19, no. 3 (September–October): 6–15.

Fellman, Anita Clair, and Michael Fellman. (1981). *Making Sense of Self: Medical Advice Literature in Late Nineteenth-Century America*. Philadelphia: U. of Pennsylvania Press.

Fischer, Hans W. (1928). *Körperschönheit und Körperkultur: Sport, Gymnastik, Tanz*. Berlin: Deutsche Buch-Gemeinschaftg.

Flint, Kate. (1993). *The Woman Reader 1837–1914*. New York: Oxford U. Press.

Garcia, Gustave. (1882). *The Actor's Art; A Practical Treatise on Stage Declamation, Public Speaking and Deportment . . .* London: T. Pettitt.

Georgen, Eleanor. (1893). *The Delsarte System of Physical Culture*. New York: Butterick Publishing Co.

Géraldy, Mme. Marie. (1893). "Lecture and Lessons Given by Mme. Géraldy (Delsarte's Daughter) in America." Unidentified translation in *Delsarte System of Oratory*, 4th ed., 533–60.

Gerber, Ellen W. (1971). *Innovators and Institutions in Physical Education*. Philadelphia: Lea & Febiger.

Giese, Fritz. (1924). *Körperseele: Gedanken über persönliche Gestaltung*. Munich: Delphin-Verlag.

Giese, Fritz, and Hedwig Hagemann, eds. (1922). *Weibliche Körperbildung und Bewegungskunst auf Grundlage des Systems Mensendieck*. Munich: Delphin-Verlag.

Giraudet, Alfred. (1885). "The Delsarte System." *Voice* 7 (January): 9–10.

———. (1895). *Mimique, physionomie et gestes; Méthode pratique, D'après le système de F. Del Sarte. Pour servir a l'expression des sentiments*. Paris: Ancienne Maison Quantin.

Glandy, Anne André. (1955). *Maxime Real del Sarte: Sa vie—sa oeuvre*. Paris: Librairie Plon.

Godwin, Joscelyn. (1986). *Music, Mysticism and Magic, A Sourcebook*. Selected and annotated by Joscelyn Godwin. London: Routledge & Kegan Paul.

———. (1994). *The Theosophical Enlightenment*. Albany: State U. of New York Press.

Godwin, Joscelyn, Christian Chanel, and John P. Deveney. (1995). *The Hermetic Brotherhood of Luxor: Initiatic and Historical Documents of an Order of Practical Occultism*. York Beach, ME: Samuel Weiser.

Goodsell, Willystine. (1923). *The Education of Women; Its Social Background and Its Problems*. New York: Macmillan.

Greenlee, Ralph Stebbins, and Robert Lemuel Greenlee. (1904). *The Stebbins Genealogy*. Chicago: McDonohue and Co.

Grotowski, Jerzy. (1969). *Towards a Poor Theater*. New York: Simon and Schuster.

Grove, Lilly. (1895). *Dancing: A Handbook of the Terpsichorean Arts in Diverse Places and Times, Savage and Civilized*. London: Longmans, Green.

Guttman, Oskar. (1882). *Gymnastics of the Voice*. New York: ESW.

———. (1884a). *Aesthetic Physical Culture; A Self-Instructor for All Cultured Circles, and Especially for Oratorical and Dramatic Artists*. Albany, NY: ESW, The Voice Press. Translated from the German. (1st ed. 1865; 2nd, rev. ed. 1879).

———. (1884b). "The Study of Dramatic Art." Part I. *Voice* 6 (November): 189–91.

———. (1885). "The Study of Dramatic Art." Part II. *Voice* 7 (March): 37–38.

Hanson, John Wesley, Jr., and Lillian Woodward Gunckel, eds. (1895). *The Delsarte Elocutionist for 1896 Containing A Practical Treatise on the Delsarte System of Physical Culture and Expression* . . . Chicago: American Publishing House.

Harang, Myra White. (1945). "The Public Career of François Delsarte." Master's thesis, LSU-BR, Department of Speech. Includes translated concert and obituary notices.

"Harmony and Expression of Motion." (1886). *The Era* (August 7): 11. Review of the Russells' Drury Lane Theatre presentation of 31 July 1886.

Hartelius, T. J. (1902). *Swedish Movements or Medical Gymnastics*. Translated by A. B. Olsen. Battle Creek, MI: Modern Medicine.

Hecht, Patsy Ann Clark. (1971). "Kinetic Techniques for the Actor: An Analysis and Comparison of the Movement Training Systems of François Delsarte, Emile Jacques-Dalcroze, and Rudolf Laban." Ph.D. diss., Wayne State U.

Hobbs, Catherine. (1995). *Nineteenth-Century Women Learn to Write*. Charlottesville: University Press of Virginia.

Hockmuth, Marie, and Richard Murphy. (1954). "Rhetorical and Elocutionary Training in Nineteenth-Century Colleges." In Wallace, 153–77.

Hodge, Francis. (1954). "The Private Theatre Schools in the Nineteenth Century." In Wallace, 552–71.

Holmström, Kirsten Gram. (1967). *Monodrama, Attitudes, Tableaux Vivants: Studies on Some Trends of Theatrical Fashion, 1770–1815*. Stockholm: Almqvist & Wiksell.

Hooper, Nettie. (1892). "Mme Géraldy in Her Paris Home Tells of Her Visit to America." *WVM* 14 (June): 159–60.

Hovey, Henrietta. [Mrs. Henrietta Crane] (1881). "The Delsarte Philosophy." Interviews with Crane and Alger). *Voice* 3 (December): 176–78.

———. [Henrietta Russell] (1891). *Yawning*. New York: United States Book Co.

Johnson, Claudia D. (1984). *American Actresses: Perspective on the Nineteenth Century*. Chicago: Nelson-Hall.

Joyeux, Odette. (1981). *Le XXe siècle de la danse*. Paris: Hachette.

Kallmeyer, Hade. (1910). *Künstlerische Gymnastik*. Schlachtensee-Berlin: Kulturverlag.

———. (1911). *Schönheit und Gesundheit des Weibes durch Gymnastik*. Schlachtensee-Berlin: Kulturverlag.

———. (1926). "Aus der Arbeit von Genevieve Stebbins." *Gymnastik* (pub. of the Deutscher Gymnastik-Bund) 1: 74–83.

Kellogg, J. H. (1905). *Ladies' Guide to Health and Disease* . . . Battle Creek, MI: Modern Medicine. (1882).

Kendall, Elizabeth. (1979). *Where She Danced*. New York: Knopf.

King, Mary Perry. (1900). *Comfort and Exercise; An Essay toward Normal Conduct*. Boston: Small, Maynard.

———. (1901). *The Basis of Beauty and Gymnasium Training for Children*. New York: Van Dyck Studios.

———. (1908). *See* Carman, Bliss, 1908.

Lämmel, Rudolf. (1928). *Der Moderne Tanz*. Berlin-Schönenberg: Peter J. Oestergaard Verlag.

Lears, T. J. Jackson. (1994). *No Place of Grace: Antimodernism and the Transformation of American Culture, 1880–1920*. Chicago: U. of Chicago Press. (1981).

Lee, Mabel. (1983). *A History of Physical Education and Sports in the U.S.A.* New York: John Wiley.

Lee, Mabel, and Bruce L. Bennett. (1960). "This Is Our Heritage: 75 Years of the American Association for Health, Physical Education and Recreation." *JOHPER* 31 (April): 25–85.

Le Favre, Carrica. (1891). *Delsartean Physical Culture with Principles of the Universal Formula*. New York: Fowler and Wells. Republished in 1892 as *Physical Culture Founded on Delsartean Principles*.

Leonard, Fred Eugene. (1927). *A Guide to the History of Physical Education*. 2nd ed. rev. by R. Tait McKenzie. Philadelphia: Lea and Febiger.

Levinson, André. (1929). "The Modern Dance in Germany." *Theatre Arts Monthly* 13 (February): 143–53.

Levy, Edwin Lewis. (1940). "Delsarte's *Cours d'esthétique appliquée*; Based on an Original Notebook." Master's thesis, LSU-BR, Department of Speech. A Delsarte pupil's notebook translated into English.

Lewis, Dio. (1862). *The New Gymnastics for Men, Women and Children*. 3rd ed. Boston: Ticknor and Fields.

"Lewis Baxter Monroe." (1889). *WVM* 11 (September): 169–70.

Linneman, William R. (1976). *Richard Hovey*. Boston: Twayne.

Locke, Ralph P. (1986). *Music, Musicians and the Saint-Simonians*. Chicago: U. of Chicago Press.

Lowell, Marion. (1895). *Harmonic Gymnastics and Pantomime Expression*. Boston: Marion Lowell.

Lumm, Emma Griffith. (1898). *The Twentieth Century Speaker* . . . Oakland, CA: Occidental Publishing Company.

Macdonald, Allan Houston. (1957). *Richard Hovey: Man and Craftsman*. Durham: Duke U. Press.

Mackaye, Mary Medberry. (n.d.). "Personal Recollections of Delsarte." Unpublished and undated manuscript, in Mackaye Archive, DCL, Box 7, Folder 12. Much of this is also quoted, sometimes with slight editing, in Percy Mackaye's *Epoch*.

———. [Mrs. Steele Mackaye] (1892). "Steele Mackaye and François Delsarte." *WVM* 14 (July): 189.

Mackaye, Percy. (1927). *Epoch: The Life of Steele Mackaye, Genius of the Theatre in Relation to His Times and Contemporaries*. 2 vols. New York: Boni and Liveright.

Mackaye, Steele. (1871). "A Plea for a Free School of Dramatic Art." Pamphlet. Mackaye Archive, DCL, Box 7, Folder 9.

———. (1875). *Philosophy of Emotion and Its Expression in Art*. Prospectus for Mackaye lectures. New York: John F. Troy and Son. Mackaye Archive, DCL, Box 7, Folder 3.

———. (1885). *Mackaye's School of Acting and Expression in Art*. Prospectus. New York: Gilliss Bros. and Turnure. Mackaye Archive, DCL, Box 7, Folder 9.

———. (1887). "Expression in Nature and Expression in Art." *Voice* 9 Part I (April): 49–51; Part II (May): 67–68; Part III (June): 82–83; Part IV (August): 121–23.

"Mackaye's School of Acting." (1885). *Voice* 7 (October): 149–50.

Makechnie, George K. (1960). "Dudley A. Sargent." *JOHPER* 31 (April): 36, 106.

Martin, John. (1936). *America Dancing*. New York: Dodge Publishing Co.; republication, New York: Dance Horizons, 1968.

Martin, Theodora Penny. (1987). *The Sound of Our Own Voices: Women's Study Clubs 1860–1910*. Boston: Beacon Press.

Mazo, Joseph H. (1977). *Prime Movers: The Makers of Modern Dance in America*. New York: William Morrow and Co.

McArthur, Benjamin. (1984). *Actors and American Culture, 1880–1920*. Philadelphia: Temple U. Press.

McCullough, Jack W. (1983). *Living Pictures on the New York Stage*. Ann Arbor, MI: UMI Research Press.

McTeague, James H. (1993). *Before Stanislavsky: American Professional Acting Schools and Acting Theory, 1875–1925*. Metuchen, NJ: The Scarecrow Press.

Meckel, Richard A. (1989). "Henrietta Russell: Delsartean Prophet to the Gilded Age." *Journal of American Culture* 12, no. 1 (Spring): 65–78.

Mensendieck, Bess M. (1908). *Körperkultur des Weibes: Praktisch hygienische und praktisch asthetische winke*. 3rd ed. Munich: F. Bruckmann, A.-G. (1906).

———. (1931). *It's Up to You*. New York: Mensendieck System Main School.

———. (1937). *The Mensendieck System of Functional Exercises* . . . Portland, ME: The Southworth-Anthoesen Press.

———. (1954). *Look Better, Feel Better: The World-Renowned Mensendieck System of Functional Movements—For a Youthful Body and Vibrant Health*. New York: Harper.

Monroe, Lewis B. (1869). *Manual of Physical and Vocal Training: For the Use of Schools and for Private Instruction*. Philadelphia: Cowperthwait and Co.

Moore, Sonia. (1967). "The Method of Physical Action." In Erika Munk, ed., *Stanislavski and America*. Greenwich, CT: Fawcett.

———. (1968). *Training an Actor: The Stanislavski System in Class*. New York: Viking.

Morgan, Anna. (1895). *An Hour with Delsarte; A Study of Expression*. Boston: Lee and Shepard.

Morris, R. Anna. (1888). *Physical Culture in the Public Schools*. Des Moines, IA: Geo. A. Miller.

———. (1891). "Delsarte Echoes from Chautauqua; II. The Religion of Physical Culture." *WVM* 13 (October): 253.

———. (1897). "Dress in Education." *WM* 20, no. 1 (September): 47–49.

Morrison, Theodore. (1974). *Chautauqua: A Center for Education, Religion, and the Arts in America*. Chicago and London: U. of Chicago Press.

"Moses True Brown." (1900). *WM* 26, no. 2 (October): 172–73.

N. A. (1893) "Genevieve Stebbins." *WM* 15 (December): 444–45.

Nadja (Beatrice Wanger), ed. (1931). *Rhythm for Humanity* . . . Paris: Herbert Clarke. Includes chapter on Delsarte by E. B. Warman.

Nast, Albert André (1947). *O mon beau printemps!*. . . . Chelles: Face a la vie. Pp. 118–33 on Giraudet, who was Nast's teacher.

National Cyclopedia of American Biography. (1891–   ) New York: J. T. White.

New York School of Expression. (1893). Prospectus announcing first season of the school. In LC.

———. (1910). 1910–1911 catalog. In the Theatre Collection of NYPL-PAC.

"The New York School of Expression" (by A. Y.). (1894). *WM* 16 (December): 464.

Newton, Stella Mary. (1974). *Health, Art and Reason: Dress Reformers of the 19th Century*. London: John Murray.

Nissen, Hartvig. (1891). *The ABC of Swedish Educational Gymnastics*. Philadelphia: F. A. Davis.

Northrop, Henry Davenport. (1895). *The Delsarte Speaker or Modern Elocution Designed Especially for Young Folks and Amateurs* . . . Philadelphia: National Publishing Co.

"Occasional Notes." (1886). *Pall Mall Gazette* (London), (June 29): 3; also printed in *The Dramatic Review* (London), (July 3): 229; and exerpts in *The Voice* 8 (October): 161. Review of the Russells' first London presentation, June 1886.

"Occasional Notes." (1886). *Pall Mall Gazette* (London), (August 2): 3–4. Review of the Russells' presentation at Drury Lane Theatre, 31 July 1886.

Odell, George C. D. (1927–1949). *Annals of the New York Stage*. 15 vols. New York: Columbia U. Press.

Odend'hal, Lucien. (1900). "Delsartiana." *WM* 25, no. 5 (July): 509.

O'Donnell, Mary P. (1936). "Gertrude Colby." *Dance Observer* (January): 1, 8.

O'Neill, Rose Meller. (1927). *The Science and Art of Speech & Gesture; A comprehensive survey of the laws of Gesture and Expression, founded on the Art and Life Work of Delsarte* . . . London: The C. W. Daniel Company.

Parker, Frank Stuart. (1887). *Order of Exercises in Elocution Given at the Cook County Normal School*. 5th ed. Chicago: Cook County Normal School.

——. (1895). "Expression of Thought through the Body." No. 1 of *Physical Culture Exercises*. Chicago: Physical Culture Extension Society.

Pendennis, Peggy. (1891). "A Craze for Delsarte: Society Leaders Who Are in Love with Its Mysteries." *New York World*, (August 16): 15.

"Phèdre in Fun." (1888). *The Era* (London) (April 21): 8.

"A Plea for Organization." (1889). *WVM* 11 (May): 96.

Polk, R. L. (1926). *Polk's Salinas, Monterey and Pacific Grove Directory*. 1st ed. San Francisco: R. L. Polk & Co.

——. (1928). *Polk's Salinas, Monterey and Pacific Grove Directory*. 2nd ed. San Francisco: R. L. Polk & Co.

——. (1930). *Polk's Salinas, Monterey, Pacific Grove and Carmel City Directory*. 3rd ed. San Francisco: R. L. Polk & Co.

——. (1933). *Polk's Salinas, Monterey, Pacific Grove and Carmel City Directory*. 4th ed. San Francisco: R. L. Polk & Co.

Porte, Alain. (1992). *François Delsarte: une anthologie*. Paris: éditions ipmc.

Potter, Helen. (1891). "Beauty and Artistic Dress." *WVM* 13 (November): 269–71; (December): 303–5.

——. (1892). "Beauty and Artistic Dress." *WVM* 14 (January): 9–11; (February): 35–38; (March): 64–66; (April): 101–102; (July): 193–94.

Preiss, Ernst. (1926). *Neue Wege der Körperkultur*. Stuttgart: Dieck & Co.

Price, Novalyne. (1941). "The Delsarte Philosophy of Expression as Seen through Certain Manuscripts of the Rev. Dr. William R. Alger." Master's thesis, LSU-BR, Department of Speech.

Rambaud, Carole, and Geneviève Vincent, eds. (1991). *François Delsarte, 1811–1871: Sources—Pensée*. Catalog for exhibition at the Museum of Toulons, 21 March–14 May 1991. Toulons: Théâtre National de la Danse et de l'Image/Chateauvallon.

Randall-Diehl, Anna. (1890). *A Practical Delsarte Primer*. Syracuse, NY: C. W. Bardeen.

Randi, Elena, ed. (1993). *François Delsarte: Le Leggi del Teatro*. Rome: Bulzoni Editore.

Ray, Harold L. (1962). "Chautauqua: Early Showcase for Physical Education." *JOHPER* 33 (November): 37–41, 69.

Renshaw, Edyth. (1954). "Five Private Schools of Speech." In Wallace, 301–25.

Robb, Mary Margaret. (1954). "The Elocutionary Movement and Its Chief Figures." In Wallace, 178–201.

Robinson, Philip. (1980). "Nourrit, Adolphe." In Stanley Sadie, ed., *The New Grove Dictionary of Music and Musicians*, 13: 431–32. London: Macmillan.

Ross, William T. (1886). *Voice Culture and Elocution*. San Francisco: Pavot, Upham & Co.

Russell, Henrietta [or Mrs. Edmund]. *See* Hovey, Henrietta.

Ruyter, Nancy Lee Chalfa. (1973). "American Delsartism: Precursor of an American Dance Art." *Educational Theatre Journal* 25 (December): 421–35.

——. (1979). *Reformers and Visionaries: The Americanization of the Art of Dance*. New York: Dance Horizons.

———. (1988). "The Intellectual World of Genevieve Stebbins." *Dance Chronicle* 11, no. 3: 389–97.

———. (1991). "Delsarte, son système et les États-Unis." Translated by Alain Porte. In Rambaud and Vincent, 33–37.

———. (1993). "Genevieve Stebbins, teorica, educatrice, artista della scena." Translated by Paola Degli Esposti. In Randi, 85–101.

———. (1996a). "Antique Longings: Genevieve Stebbins and American Delsartean Performance." In Susan Leigh Foster, ed., *Corporealities: Dancing, Knowledge, Culture and Power*, 70–89. London: Routledge.

———. (1996b). "The Delsarte Heritage." *Dance Research* (London) 14, no. 1 (Summer): 62–74.

St. Denis, Ruth. (1939). *An Unfinished Life: An Autobiography*. New York: Harper and Brothers.

Sanburn, Frederick, ed. (1890). *A Delsartean Scrapbook: Health, Personality, Beauty, House Decoration, etc*. With Preface by Walter Crane. 11th ed. New York: Lovell, Gestefeld.

Sargent, Dudley Allen. (1904). *Health, Strength & Power*. New York: H. M. Caldwell.

———. (1906). *Physical Education*. Boston: Ginn & Company. Anthology of his writings since the early 1880s.

———. (1927). *Dudley Allen Sargent: An Autobiography*. Edited by Ledyard W. Sargent. Philadelphia: Lea & Febiger.

Sargent, Franklin H. (1890). "The Silent Art; A Study of Pantomine and Action." *WVM* 12, Part I (January): 11–13; Part II (February): 45; Part III (March): 68–69; Part IV (April): 95–96; Part V (May): 127–28; Part VI (June): 152–54; Part VII (July): 181–82; Part VIII (September): 217–19; Part IX (October): 246–48; Part X (November): 275–77.

———. (1891). "The Silent Art; A Study of Pantomime and Action." *WVM* 13, Part XI (March): 65–68.

Shaver, Claude L. (1954). "Steele Mackaye and the Delsarte Tradition." In Wallace, 202–18.

Shawn, Ted. (1974). *Every Little Movement; A Book about François Delsarte*. Republication of 2nd rev. & enl. ed. of 1963. New York: Dance Horizons.

Shelton, Suzanne. (1978). "The Influence of Genevieve Stebbins on the Early Career of Ruth St. Denis." In Dianne L. Woodruff, ed., *Essays in Dance Research from the Fifth CORD Conference, Philadelphia, November 11–14, 1976*, 33–49. Dance Research Annual IX. New York: Congress on Research in Dance.

———. (1981). *Divine Dancer: A Biography of Ruth St. Denis*. Garden City, NY: Doubleday and Co.

Shoemaker, Mrs. J. W. (1891). *Delsartean Pantomimes with Recital and Musical Accompaniment*. Philadelphia: Penn Publishing Company.

Smith-Baranzini, Marlene. (1998). Introduction to *The Shirley Letters from the California Mines, 1851–1852* by Louise Amelia Knapp Smith Clappe. Berkeley: Heyday Books.

Smith-Rosenberg, Carroll. (1986). *Disorderly Conduct: Visions of Gender in Victorian America*. New York: Oxford U. Press.

Solomon, Barbara M. (1985). *In the Company of Educated Women: A History of Women and Higher Education in America*. New Haven: Yale U. Press.

Sorell, Walter. (1986). *Dance in Its Time*. New York: Columbia U. Press.

Southwick, F. Townsend. (1890). "Questions in Delsartism." *WVM* 12 (November): 281–82.

———. (1893). "What is the Delsarte System." *WM* 15 (June): 193–94.

———. (1893–1894). "Topics of the Month: A Criticism of Current Elocutionary Literature." *WM* 15 and 16. Column appeared frequently from October 1893 to December 1894.

———. (1897). *Elocution and Action*. 3rd ed., rev. & enl. New York: ESW (1890). Sections published in *WVM*, October 1889 to September 1890.

———. (1900). *Steps to Oratory: A School Speaker*. New York: American Book Company.

Spears, Betty. (1986). *Leading the Way: Amy Morris Homans and the Beginnings of Professional Education for Women*. Westport, CT: Greenwood.

Stanley, Gregory Kent. (1996). *The Rise and Fall of the Sportswoman: Women's Health, Fitness, and Athletics, 1860–1940*. New York: Peter Lang.

Stebbins, Genevieve. (1885). *Delsarte System of Expression*. See 1902.

———. (1886). "Foot-Light Studies." *Voice* 8 (January): 14–15. Review of a Shakespeare production.

———. (1887). "François Delsarte." In Wilbor 1887: 258–61.

———. (1888). *Society Gymnastics and Voice Culture, Adapted from the Delsarte System*. New York: ESW.

———. (1893). *Dynamic Breathing and Harmonic Gymnastics*. New York: ESW.

———. (1895). *Genevieve Stebbins Drills*. New York: ESW.

———. (1901). *An Egyptian Initiation by Iamblichus, a Neo-Platonist of the 4th century*. Trans. into French from the original by P. Christian; trans. from French to English by Genevieve Stebbins Astley in 1901. Denver, CO: Edward Leon Bloom, 1965.

———. (1902). *Delsarte System of Expression*. 6th ed. New York: ESW. (1885). In some references, the early editions are referred to as *The Delsarte System of Dramatic Expression*. The 2nd (1887), 3rd (1889), and 4th (1891) editions include Delsarte's address before the Philotechnic Society. The 6th edition also includes several new sections. Reprint New York: Dance Horizons, 1977. All citations in the text refer to this edition, but it should be kept in mind that much of the writing in it had appeared earlier.

———. (1913a). *The Genevieve Stebbins System of Physical Training*. enl. ed. New York: ESW. (1898).

———, ed. (1913b). *The Quest of the Spirit by a Pilgrim of the Way*. New York: ESW; London: Henry J. Glaisher.

Taylor, George Henry. (1860). *An Exposition of the Swedish Movement-Cure . . .* New York: Fowler and Wells.

———. (1871). *Diseases of Women; Their Causes, Prevention, and Radical Cure*. Philadelphia: Geo. Maclean.

———. (1879a). *Health by Exercise Showing What Exercises to Take and How to Take Them to Remove Special Physical Weakness . . .* New York: Fowler & Wells. A reprint of the 1860 volume with an added section on massage.

———. (1879b). *Health for Women. . . . With Full Directions for Self-Treatment*. New York: American Book Exchange.

———. (1885). *Pelvic and Hernial Therapeutics. Principles and Methods for Remedying Chronic Affections of the Lower Part of the Trunk, Including Processes for Self-Cure*. New York: John B. Alden.

Tels, Ellen. [née Ellen Knipper Rabeneck] (1935). "Le Système du Geste selon Françqis Delsarte." *Archives Internationales de la Danse*. 3rd year, Special Number (1 November): 6–7.

Terry, Walter. (1969). *Miss Ruth; The "More Living Life" of Ruth St. Denis*. New York: Dodd, Mead.

Thomas, Fannie Edgar. (1892). "What Philadelphia Teachers Think of Mme. Géraldy's Visit." *WVM* 14 (May): 138–39.

Thomas, Helen. (1995). *Dance, Modernity and Culture*. London and New York: Routledge.

Thomas, Julia, and Annie Thomas. (1892). *Thomas Psycho-Physical Culture*. New York: ESW.

Thompson, Mary S. (1892a). *Rhythmical Gymnastics: Vocal and Physical*. New York: ESW.

———. (1892b). "Reminiscences of Lewis B. Monroe." *WVM* 14 (February): 38–39.

———. (1892c). "The Relation of Gymnastics to Expression." Part II of "Delsartism in America." *WVM* 14 (March): 60–61.

———. (1892d). "The Delsarte Philosophy and System of Expression." *WVM* 14 (November): 323–24.

———. (1897). "Expression or Repression? The Battle between the Anglo-Saxon and Latin Races in Art-Development. A Critique on the New York Convention of the National Association of Elocutionists." *WM* 19 (August): 764–74.

Toepfer, Karl. (1997). *Empire of Ecstasy: Nudity and Movement in German Body Culture, 1910–1935*. Berkeley: U. of California Press.

Van Dalen, Deobold B., Elmer D. Mitchell, and Bruce L. Bennett. (1953). *A World History of Physical Education: Cultural. Philosophical. Comparative*. Englewood Cliffs, NJ: Prentice-Hall.

Vance, Lee J. (1892). "The Evolution of the Dance." *Popular Science Monthly* 41 (October): 739–56.

Volkonsky, Prince Sergei Mikhailovich. (1913). *Vyrazitel'nyi chelovek, Stsenicheskoe vospitanie zhesta. Po Delsarte-u. S illyustratsiyami so statui i kartin starinnykh masterov*. (Expressive man. Teaching gesture for the stage. After Delsarte. With illustrations from statues and pictures by old masters.) St. Petersburg: Izdanie "Apollona."

Wallace, Karl R., ed. (1954). *History of Speech Education in America*. New York: Appleton-Century-Crofts.

Warman, Edward Barrett. (1883). "Elocutionary Training. Objected to by the Editor of a Religious Journal, but Defended." *Voice* 5 (May): 72–73.

———. (1892). *Gestures and Attitudes. An Exposition of the Delsarte Philosophy of Expression, Practical and Theoretical*. Boston: Lee and Shepard.

———. (1896). "Speaking, Reading and Singing. Fundamental Principles Necessary to Obtain the Best Vocal Results." *WM* 18. First Paper (January): 19–22; Second Paper (February): 114–18.

———. (1931). "Delsarte, His Life and Philosophy." In Nadja, 51–76.

Wayne, John J. (1993). "Little Egypt—Full Circle." *Arabesque* 19, no. 3 (September–October): 18–21.

Welch, Paula D., and Harold A. Lerch. (1981). *History of American Physical Education and Sport*. Springfield, IL: Charles C. Thomas.

Werner, Edgar S. (1889). "The Late Oscar Guttman." *WVM* 21 (June): 101–102.

———. (1892a). "Delsartism in America, Part I." *WVM* 14 (March): 59–60.

———. [E.S.W.] (1892b). "Interview with Mr. F. Townsend Southwick." *WVM* 14 (May): 140.

———. [E.S.W.] (1892c). "Discussion at the March Meeting of the N.Y. Association of Teachers of Oratory." *WVM* 14 (May): 140–41.

———. [E.S.W.] (1892d). "Interview with Mme. Gérardy in New York." *WVM* 14 (June): 160–161.

———. (1896). "History of the National Association of Elocutionists." *WM* 18 (June): 489–519.

Who's Who in America. 1899–1900 and continuing.

Wilbor, Elsie M., ed. (1887). *Werner's Directory of Elocutionists, Readers, Lecturers and Other Public Instructors and Entertainers*. New York: ESW.

———. (1888). "Real vs. Artificial Feeling." *Voice* 10 (March): 37–38.

———. (1889). "The Spread of Delsartism" (interview with Edmund Russell). *WVM* 11 (May): 90–92.

———. (1890). "Chautauqua." *WVM* 12 (August): 194.

———. (1891). "Delsarte Methods; A Glimpse of the Work of Mrs. Genevieve Stebbins Thompson." *WVM* 13, no. 2 (February): 29–31. Slightly edited version republished as addendum to Stebbins 1902.

———. (1892). "Ling-Delsarte." *WVM* 14 (June): 181.

———. (1894). "Genevieve Stebbins's Matinee." *WM* 16 (February): 69.

———. (1895). "New York School of Expression." *WM* 17 (October): 782–84.

———, ed. (1905). *Delsarte Recitation Book*. 4th ed., enl. New York: ESW. (1889). 4th ed. reprinted as part of Granger Index Reprint Series. Freeport, NY: Books for Libraries Press, 1971.

Wilson, Garff B. (1966). *A History of American Acting*. Bloomington: Indiana U. Press.

Woodward, Adèle M. (1893). "Delsarte's Daughter in America." In *Delsarte System of Oratory*, 561–65.

Woody, Thomas. (1929). *A History of Women's Education in the United States*. New York: The Science Press.

Young, William C. (1975). *Famous Actors and Actresses on the American Stage; Documents of American Theatre History*. New York and London: R. R. Bowker and Co.

Zorn, John W., ed. (1968). *The Essential Delsarte*. Metuchen, NJ: The Scarecrow Press. Reprinted in somewhat edited form from *Delsarte System of Oratory*: sections of Delsarte's writings, the Durivage 1871 *Atlantic Monthly* article, report of Mme. Géraldy's visit, and the Delaumosne book.

Index

About the Author

NANCY LEE CHALFA RUYTER is Professor of Dance at the University of California, Irvine.

ISBN 0-313-31042-4

90000>

EAN

9 780313 310423

HARDCOVER BAR CODE